# You can Learn to be Happy

A Practical, Rational Approach to Happiness!

Thota Ramesh

## Other books by the Author

(Available at www.amazon.com)

**"Teamwork & Indian Culture"**

A Practical Guide for Working with Indians

**"Daily Life in Indian Culture"**

An Insightful Guide to Customs & Traditions of India

Revised Edition - 2024

**ISBN-13:** 979-8886842098

Imprint: Independently published

# Dedication

To three family members
whose unconditional love
has no limits:

1. My mother – The late Mrs. Agamma
2. My sister – Mrs. Jayaprada
3. My sister-in-law – Mrs. Leela

# CONTENTS

***Before enlightenment***
***chop wood, carry water.***

***After enlightenment,***
***chop wood, carry water.***

**- Zen saying**

# Prologue

It is unfortunate that despite great strides in human evolution, we have been struggling to live happily. Many great thinkers tried their best to communicate ways to a happy life, but it has not been understood well. During my search, I have found the answers to "What do we need to do to live happily?" in spiritual teachings; and answers to "How to attain that happiness?" in modern Psychology. By applying the knowledge of ancient wisdom combined with the techniques of modern Psychology, I have learned to live happily.

I believe every problem in this world, including gaining happiness, can be solved by applying scientific principles. I have applied the rational approach to solving the problem of being happy. It helped me understand the world we live in, the beauty of nature, the greatness of our mind, and its power over us. In this book, I am going to share how we can garner the power of our minds to stay happy. Once the logic behind the phenomenon is understood well, it becomes easy to comprehend, and you get confidence. It needs practice, but you know you can master it confidently and joyfully.

A particular event in my life has forced me to investigate what life is all about. At the age of 22 years, I got my master's degree in business administration. Like any middle-class person, my life's ambition, at that time, was to get a good job. 22 years of my life were spent preparing for that day. Luckily, my efforts paid off and I got a job as a software programmer. I felt I had done everything that had to be done in life.

**What Should I Do Now?**

Suddenly, the question of "WHAT should I do now?" came up. Many options were suggested to me - excelling in the profession, getting married, going for higher studies, going abroad, etc.

It would have been better (I felt that way at that time) if I was satisfied with "WHAT". But then the question of "WHY?" came up. This led me to the basic question of "**What is the ultimate purpose of our life?**" Or in other words "**What are we supposed to do with our life?**"

I started thinking about the purpose of life, and it appeared then that there was no purpose. But one thing was clear to me; terminating life cannot be life's purpose as it is a contradiction. So, I concluded that maintaining life, if not the basic purpose, is one of the important functions of life. It was evident from the great mechanisms provided by NATURE to animals (including us) and plants to protect and continue life. It is fascinating to see how complex the behaviors of males and females (of all species) have been shaped to FORCE them to reproduce. The mating rituals of some of the species, including fish, are mind-blowing (Watch the movie "Animals Are Beautiful People" to see nature in action).

So, as I took it for granted that continuation of life is important, I decided to see what essential things are required for it. First, anything that goes against the continuation of life should be discouraged and avoided. Next, nurture the things required for the continuation of life, broadly:

- Physiological needs have to be satisfied and
- psychological needs to be met.

As the state of happiness is an indication of well-being, "being HAPPY" turns out to be the purpose of life.

<u>**Note:**</u> If a person is happy by not taking food, in other words not trying to maintain his life, then that is against nature. That should be discouraged.

This process of thinking led me to conclude that the ultimate purpose of life is to be happy. And I have started investigating how my happiness gets affected and how I can gain control over it.

Let me digress a little here. When it comes to happiness, many people resort to religious and spiritual practices/rituals. If you are very religious & believe in GOD, and if the religious practices seem to give you some solace, please continue with them. The ideas that I am going to share in this book will not interfere with your religious or spiritual practices. You can continue to practice what you believe.

I promise you that this book will give you a significant improvement in your happiness, assuming you apply the learnings from this book. We lost our natural ability to be happy as we grew up. Once we understand what has gone wrong and realize it, the path to happiness becomes joyful and easy. Contrary to popular perception, being happy is the ONLY thing that can be under our FULL control. You are the master of YOUR happiness. The key to happiness is in YOUR hands. This book will guide you to gain that CONTROL.

The good news is that there is no need for us to escape from our responsibilities or take up a spiritual journey to find happiness. I am a family man, and I have consciously practiced control using **a simple technique** that I am going to share with you in this book. It made all the difference. **Applying this technique is easy** - but how quickly, and to what extent you will learn to be happy depends entirely on YOU.

Irrespective of your age, you can start learning to be happy. It is never too late. I guarantee you increased happiness within a short time of applying this technique. As per the Pareto principle of 80-20, you will gain 80% results with 20% effort. And you will realize that the small controls you gain make a great difference to your happiness and your life.

**To get the best out of this book:**

Become a learner, have a child-like attitude, and take charge.

1. Read each chapter in the given order.
2. After reading a chapter, set the book aside, think about the ideas communicated and internalize them.

Be open; do not accept blindly everything that I say. Think about them, deliberate, and accept those that work for you. Best wishes!

---***--

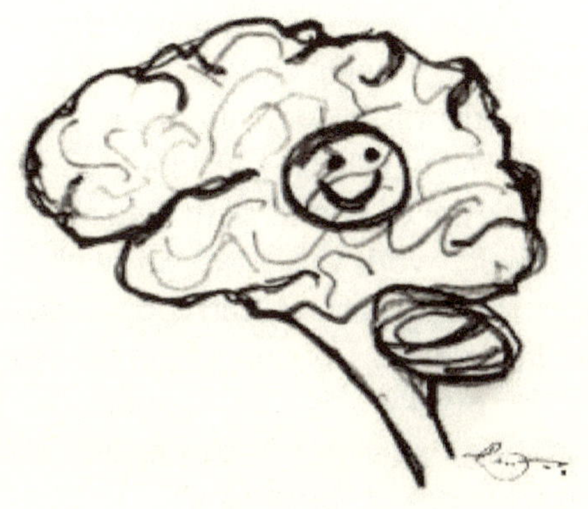

# Chapter #1
# About YOUR Happiness

Before we move on to your happiness, let us look at human beings in general. We are born free, and our natural behavior is to love and stay happy. You can see that in children. Observe any child, almost all of them appear to be happy irrespective of the environment around them. As we grow up, we learn lots of different things and we get conditioned to respond in a particular way. To go back to your original state of 'Happy and loving' being you need to undo all those learnings. In psychology, it is referred to as deconditioning.

When we observe animals, it appears they stay happy almost all the time. They get into violent behavior only when it affects their survival or their mating opportunity. At that time the instinct of "fight or flight" gets triggered. At the end of the incident that led to a "fight or flight" response, you will have a winner and a loser. That is the typical outcome of animal behavior. We human beings, being endowed with a larger brain and the immense power of thinking, can get a wide variety of outcomes than just "Win or Lose". The outcomes can be anywhere on the spectrum of Win to Lose. The most preferred outcome that we should work for is a "Win-Win". And this is possible only for human beings as we can cooperate effectively compared to other living beings. If you notice, the reason for all the achievements of mankind is this cooperative behavior. Yuval Noah Harari has explained it beautifully in his book “Homo Deus: A brief history of Tomorrow”.

Now, let us look at a few situations, and how they play out. After going through these case studies, think of unhappy events that you have encountered. See if you could have done something different.

**Case 1:**

I say that you are DUMB, IGNORANT, and LACKING common sense; and because of that, you are struggling to be happy.

What do you say?

In all probability, you may get ANGRY and FURIOUS about my accusations that you are dumb and lack common sense. And you may be feeling insulted and may even be thinking of putting this book down. Wait a second!

I did that to demonstrate a point! *My apologies to you for causing this feeling.* [In case you are not offended, congratulations! You did not allow my words to hurt you. Please read along.]

Did you notice what happened to you? Your body might have shown symptoms related to anger. You might have felt the discomfort. Just by saying a few words, I made you feel a little unhappy. In other words, I have taken away your happiness.

**Notice this:**
***In this situation, your happiness was controlled by me.***

You gave me the Control Switch. This is the FIRST thing you should realize. A person like me, no way related to you, no way can get in touch with you, probably you may not see me in your ENTIRE life... to this guy... you gave YOUR happiness Control Switch.

But, in reality...

> Who has your happiness Control Switch?
> Who made you angry?
> Who made you unhappy?

It is definitely not me. So, who made you unhappy? It is YOU. You decided to get hurt by my words. You allowed yourself to get angry. You CHOSE to be unhappy.

I have used the word "CHOSE", indicating that you had various choices, but you preferred the negative one. But in reality, you are CONDITIONED to react to it in this particular way. That means, you automatically reacted. You were no longer analyzing and deciding what was good for you.

There are two things we can learn from this. First, your emotions, thus your happiness, is in YOUR Control. The second one, most of your behavior is CONDITIONED. From the day you are born to date, you have been conditioned by your family, friends, and society.

***The effect of conditioning is so powerful that it immobilizes you in many ways.***

**Case 2:**

I know a friend who has a special place in his heart for one of his wristwatches. He always wants to put on that particular watch on special and important occasions, without fail. One day, he had an important meeting and could not find that watch. He was very upset and showed his annoyance at his wife and kids. Not only his mood was bad, but it also made everyone get into a bad mood. As you might expect, his meeting did not go well. Not wearing that watch made him worry, and consequently it resulted in unhappiness for him and others.

What happened here?

Again, CONDITIONING! Somehow – call it superstition or another thing – he got conditioned to believe in that way. Not just this, many people FEEL very bad if they are unable to find their favorite things or unable to use them or something happens to those things. Say for example – a favorite pen, favorite furniture or decorative item, favorite car, etc. Any damage to this favorite thing, or loss of it will make people very unhappy. This is called "ATTACHMENT" – a result of conditioning.

Am I saying not to take care of your favorite things? No! Not at all.

Take care of them, protect them, and enjoy doing that. But do not lose your happiness if some damage happens to them. Do not attach your happiness to them. And be prepared to LOSE everything. In this world, you can/may lose...

- your money
- your job
- your prestige
- your social status
- even the LOVE and AFFECTION of your family and friends

They are NOT fully under your control.

***The only things that you can take under your COMPLETE control are:***

- ***your mind***
- ***thus, your emotions***
- ***thus, your happiness***

So, the only time you can feel unhappy is when you have physical pain or discomfort. Whenever you are unhappy – just check if you have any physical discomfort. See what is causing that physical discomfort/pain and try your best to remove the cause.

Do you agree?

But there is something interesting about physical pain. Let us explore. Even in the case of experiencing pain, your mind plays a significant role. For a moment, go back to your childhood. Recollect the incident when you got hurt badly while playing your favorite sport say Soccer or Basketball. Probably, you did not feel any pain until the game was over. Only when someone pointed it out or only when you were washing your body, you would realize that you got hurt.

Correct?

What happened here? Your mind made you ignore the pain. And the most interesting point here is that, if someone asked you whether you would risk yourself hurting again, you would have said "ABSOLUTELY! I enjoy all of it – playing, getting hurt, and everything."

Look at movie stars such as Jackie Chan, and Shah Rukh Khan of India; and sports stars such as Soccer hero Neymar and Indian Cricket legend Sachin Tendulkar. They had multiple bone fractures and many injuries all over the body. But they could withstand that pain and continue to take risks and enjoy what they do. Given a chance, they would avoid this type of injury. But they physically exert themselves in their work so much that the amount of pain it causes cannot be measured. For them going through this pain is joy and happiness. How you look at pain is again in your mind i.e. under YOUR control.

The control your mind can exert on your body is tremendous. Medical research has proved time and again that you can improve your well-being just by being positive and believing in yourself. The medical community has recognized the role of the mind over the body. And for many serious illnesses such as Heart attack, Cancer, etc. they are working on the minds of patients while treating their bodies.

**Case 3:**

Let us look at one more example that involves physical as well as mental effort. Let us analyze how our happiness is affected.

> Someone uses foul language against you, with venom. As far as the physical effort is concerned, you are just listening, but the other guy is going through a multitude of changes in his body and mind. In real physical terms, he is experiencing more pain than you (as long as you don't allow your MIND to react in a negative way). If you want to control him, go ahead, and do whatever is necessary including physically hurting the other person. But do it without experiencing the negative effects of anger.

Any time you feel unhappy or have a bad mood, just check whether there is any physical discomfort. If not, there is no need to be unhappy. Measure the situation only in terms of real physical effort. And this book is about how to gain control of the mind to live happily. Let us now look at what life is all about - off to the next chapter.

---***---

# Chapter #2
# Cross the 7 steps

- Have you ever wondered what this life is all about?
- Did you try finding out what is the meaning or purpose of life?
- Did you hear people talking about "Meaningful life"?

They are tough ideas to comprehend. They do not have any concrete explanations. It is all intriguing. As we start thinking deeply about them, we may end up in confusion and sometimes it may lead to depression.

Just think about the Universe. Take time out and spend a few minutes gazing into the night sky. You will realize how insignificant we are in this whole Universe. It is a little depressing as well as astonishing to know about the Universe.

Please pay attention and follow these statements: We all learned that our Earth is part of the Solar system, and the planets go around the Sun. (And this Solar system is part of the Milky Way Galaxy.) The Sun is one of the several ***hundred billion stars*** that exist in the Milky Way Galaxy. The Milky Way Galaxy is one among 120 ***billion Galaxie***s in the observable Universe. Beyond this observable Universe, called the Cosmological Horizon, the Universe is still expanding.

In brief, like our Sun there are ***10,000 million, million, million stars*** in this Universe. Mind-blowing, right?

Coming back to this earth you are one among the 6 billion people in this world. Our species, by one estimate, is one among 8.7 million species on this planet. If you want to count the number of living organisms, it will be another mind-boggling number. In this whole Cosmic world (Universe), we are just a speck. Added to this, when we compare our life span to the life of the Universe, it is once again minuscule. Knowing these facts forces us to wonder what the meaning of life is.

## The Meaning/Purpose of Life

I have gone through many interpretations of the "Meaning of life". I studied how people try to search for or find the "Meaning of life". People who claim to have found their purpose would suddenly become calm and get busy with their lives. Their paths may not be the same, but each might have found their **awakening**. But the underlying theme is that it keeps them busy. It gives the individual a goal. It convinces them to focus on a particular thing. ***It helps them fill their time.*** Many people feel LOST if they do not have a specific goal. So, people come up with fancy ways of describing it as the "Meaning of life". The truth is that we all need a way to structure/spend the time given to us by our lives.

I found a very interesting theory about how we structure/spend our time. Dr. Eric Berne, the founder of Transactional Analysis, suggests that we structure time in six different ways.

1. **Withdrawal**: spending time in isolation without any contact with others.
2. **Rituals:** Polite exchanges which are highly structured, say greetings.
3. **Pastimes:** Talking about predictable subjects without engaging in any action.
4. **Activities:** Working towards a goal.
5. **Games:** A sequence of interactions with others that end up with both parties experiencing familiar bad feelings.
6. **Intimacy:** Honest exchanges with shared openness, and trust. (This word "Intimacy" has a special meaning here. Do not get confused with the romantic meaning of intimacy.)

I suggest you read more about this. A good amount of material is available on the Internet. It will help you realize how you are structuring your time. The following two observations helped me understand life better:

- the place of our existence in the Universe
- the so-called meaning of life

With these in mind, I have identified 7 ideas that you need to ponder over systematically and internalize them for you to move forward. As I said earlier, please do not blindly believe what I communicate here. Take your time, think meticulously, and come to your conclusions. I call these 7 ideas, the 7 steps. Each idea leads to the next idea. You must cross these steps carefully with a thorough understanding.

## Step 1

### All Living Beings - Humans, Animals, Plants, including Insects - are Equal.

Compared to all other species on the Earth, we have larger brains, and we are more cooperative. Due to that, we have created many wonders. But that does not take away the greatness of all other species. They are great in their own world and their ways. Just watch nature closely. You will be amazed to see the wonders they create. For example, some of the birds' nests are so complicated and beautiful that we cannot fully comprehend their intricacies. To my knowledge, no human being can create such a nest, even with all the technology and intelligence that we have.

From the Universe's perspective, we have already seen how insignificant our life is. If you compare us with animals, many animals are much more powerful and humongous than us. The more you understand the world of these animals and other living things, the humbler you will become. The differences that we perceive among all these living beings appear superficial, and we realize how each life is great in its own way. Concerning the gigantic Universe having 10,000 trillion Galaxies (including the Galaxies beyond the observable Universe), we can say all the living things on this Earth are equal in the perspective of nature.

## Step 2

### Nature Demands that We Live Our Full-life and Allow Our Species to Continue.

A close observation of nature reveals that every living being is genetically coded to fight for its survival and its species' survival. Thanks to the great nature videographers and filmmakers, we can watch the fascinating world of all living things. They have captured elegantly how every living organism develops unique strategies for its survival. It includes plants and insects. Not only do they protect themselves, but all of them also go to great extents to protect their offspring. The strategies they devise to ward off a predator, the cunning ways they adopt to distract & deceive them, the unique techniques they use to train their younger ones - all these traits make them great in their worlds.

The most amazing part of life is that of procreation. Nature has devised highly complex mechanisms for this process. Take a plant in a desert, and trace the path of its seeds getting protected, transported, and germinated. Many other species in nature play a collaborative role in making this happen. It is just unfathomable. In the case of insects and animals, nature has devised very complicated beautiful ways to get the male and female to mate.

Nature is communicating loud and clear that every living organism should Live – Protect - Procreate. ***For any reason, if you cannot procreate you can help protect our species by contributing to the welfare of others.***

## Step 3

### Being Happy is the Ultimate Purpose of life.

As discussed above, the ultimate purpose is to live and let your species live. There are many sects, and religions which discuss the afterlife; and they propose causal links between the current life, the past, and the future lives. Whether you believe it or not is your choice. If you believe in the afterlife and their causal relationships, you may choose the activities that might help you with that goal. But, irrespective of your beliefs, you will agree with me that staying happy is a good choice. Anyone who lives happily, without causing unhappiness to others, has served the purpose of his life.

In general, being happy is an indication of the positive health of a living being, and it helps in the continuation of life. So, for all practical purposes, decide to stay happy and focus on learning how to be happy. Deciding to live every moment happily is an important step on the path to lifelong happiness.

## Step 4

### Realize that the Root Cause of Your Unhappiness is Your Mind.

Though all living beings are equal as per Step #1, human beings are bestowed with a powerful mind that has helped us build the world we live in. Unfortunately, this very powerful mind is the root cause of our unhappiness. The ability to think about the past and future has made many of us unhappy - mainly worrying about the past or anxious about the future. It appears that other species do not have this problem as they act as per their instincts and live in the present.

Usually, many of us spend our present time making our future happy. When the future becomes present, that time is also spent on making further future happy; and the process continues. Thus, we end up eternally working for future happiness. In the end, we may not have time to live happily.

As we can mull over the PAST and the FUTURE, we spend our present time worrying about the things that happened and that are going to happen. Mind it, you are not worrying about the PRESENT, you are spending the present time worrying about the past or future. Choose wisely and try to live in the present. We should apply the knowledge we have acquired in the past, to live comfortably and happily in the present. Rather than worrying about the future, we should plan for the future, and decide what we have to do in the present.

In short, we should remember the following 3 steps.

1. Learn from the PAST
2. Plan for the FUTURE
3. Live in the PRESENT

Let us look at an imaginary dreadful scenario to understand this:

**The Situation:** We are caught by some terrorists/killers. They have aimed their guns at us within point-blank range. They are ready to shoot us at any time.

**Typical Reaction**: We would be terrified. We would be shivering with the fear of death and might start experiencing trauma. And we may also lose control over our senses.

**The Preferred Reaction**: If we follow the above 3 steps.

- Being killed is the FUTURE.
- Caught and gun pointed at us is PRESENT.

As far as the present is concerned there is nothing to worry about. The worry is only about the FUTURE event of being killed. So, our thinking should go this way:

If we are "shot at", we will experience the pain and the trauma. That is inevitable ***if*** we are shot. At present, we should plan for the future i.e., how to save ourselves. As per that plan, take the necessary action required at present. Our goal is to save ourselves from these bad people. So, we should think of a solution and implement it.

Experiencing the trauma at present is meaningless and useless. This trauma is in ***addition*** to the trauma we are going to experience when we are shot. So, let us try to minimize our suffering. Because of this attitude, we may hit upon a solution and save our lives.

The other possibility is that the terrorists may not be thinking of killing us at all. They might just want to frighten us. In that case, all the worries/suffering and thinking that we will be shot are useless. And not only that, this suffering from fear itself may be worse than the actual suffering we might experience when we are shot at. For all you know, we might get instant death when we are shot, and may not even have time to experience the pain.

After rational thinking, if we feel that appearing scared or afraid makes them stop their actions, then we should lessen all our control and feign scared.

## Step 5

### No Work is Inferior. Enjoy Every Task You Do. And, Do it to the Best of Your Ability.

Work, one of the 6 ways of time-structuring, is the most favorite option for many of us. Apart from accomplishing some goals, it takes care of our need to fill time. To stay happy, it is important to recognize that no work is inferior. We should respect every task as long as it serves some purpose and adds value.

Consider these tasks:

- Doing your office work
- A simple act of playing a game with a child
- Getting dirty doing gardening
- Cooking a dish
- Repairing an old item
- Polishing shoes
- Washing clothes
- Giving a sponge bath to a patient
- Mopping the floor etc.,

All the above tasks are meant to accomplish some goals. But some of them are enjoyable and some are not so enjoyable. Why? The word "work" invokes feelings of drudgery, effort, boredom, tiredness, etc. Ask a child to do work and ask the same child to play. You get completely opposite reactions. It is mostly the same with many of us.

Work can be Physical or Mental. Physical work is easy to recognize, but many fail to notice the mental work. I remember one incident; one day the lady who mops the floor in our office asked me "Sir, what work is being done in this office? I don't see anyone doing any work except sitting and looking at those small TVs (referring to the Computer monitors)". In her world, work is doing something physical. The dictionary defines work as "physical or mental activity undertaken to achieve a purpose." Play is also cited as one form of work.

So, the question now is, how come people ENJOY 'playing', but not other types of 'Work'? For example, ask your son or younger brother to get you a glass of water. He might do this task grudgingly and may feel it is drudgery. The same kid would run like hell on the Soccer field or on the Cricket field to get the ball. And interestingly, at the end of the game, he feels good about it and looks forward to playing again. If you purely go by the physics definition i.e., the amount of energy spent, the effort made, etc., playing Soccer/Cricket is more Work than getting you a glass of water. In a strict sense, more energy was spent on playing and more effort was made. But... the feeling of joy and being happy is more. The key factor here is the MIND. It does not matter how much more or less energy is spent, what matters is how you THINK about the activity.

It is our attitude/feeling toward the activity that makes the activity interesting, and enjoyable. Similarly, a negative attitude makes other activities drudgery, menial, and tedious, and makes us feel exhausted.

> *More than the amount of energy spent, it is our mindset that makes us feel tired, exhausted, and unhappy.*

Take any sports person or entertainer e.g., Neymar and Jackie Chan, they love their work. Even though they have amassed enormous wealth and fame they continue to exert themselves. And you agree with me that they are enjoying every bit of it, even though playing Soccer, Martial arts, and acting is their work.

It makes sense to enjoy our work whatever we do to earn a living. After all, we spend a good part of our time on this. It is futile to think that 'we can choose a job that we love'. Enjoying work is enjoying most of our life. We need to look at various ways of getting a kick out of it. One of the best ways is to focus on improving whatever we do and set challenges for ourselves. Just like in a game, having clear-cut goals and achieving them will give immense joy. By enjoying work, we become more focused and more productive. It makes the individual achieve his goals such as having healthy relationships, taking care of family, excelling in his profession, etc.

As such the human body is meant for physical and mental work. From the caveman days to now, the need for physical activity has reduced gradually and the need for mental activities has increased. But exercising both physical and mental capabilities is the way to happiness and joy.

So, start enjoying work and enjoying life.

## Step 6

### Be Open. Let Others Know You.

Be open about you and your ideas. Being open, objective, and logical is the first step towards understanding life in its real sense. This mindset is the hallmark of scientists and philosophers. All the luxuries and the quality of life we have today are due to this thinking. It is unfortunate that when it comes to happiness and personal success, people tend to ignore logic.

Each one of us is unique in our own way. Our family background and the environment we grew up in contribute to what we are today. So, many times our thoughts and actions may not be in sync with what others expect. This can cause stress and might force us to suppress information about ourselves and our ideas. If this continues, we will be forced to conform to the existing majority norms. In the short-term, it might help us face life with a little ease; but in the long run, it would become a major hindrance to our growth.

The first step towards happiness is accepting yourself as you are. Let everyone know about you, your thoughts, and actions. Break the shackles of concealing. For example, many teenagers are overly concerned about their physical appearance. It is normal during that phase, but if it continues beyond that age, it could become a serious problem. I had a similar problem at that age. I am short, and till I accepted that fact, it was a constant issue bugging me. Some of the facts people tend to hide or wish to conceal are related to:

- Physical appearance
- Family background
- Poor financial status
- Family problems

- Children's academic progress, intelligence levels
- Etc...

Many people go to a great extent to hide the above-mentioned information. As a result, these people will not be able to share their personal feelings openly. It can lead to the bottling up of negative emotions, as well as not seeking help. Usually, these people are afraid of the possibility of negative reactions, the possibility of accepting an opposing view, and the possibility of changing their ways of living. They are comfortable with their habits. Doing away with those habits is a scary thing for them. Thus, they become victims of their old habits. Instead of the freedom to experience new situations, they get confined to their restricted world. Referring to the 6 ways of structuring time, these people avoid spending time in "Intimacy"; instead, they prefer "Pastimes". Thus, if you are not open to sharing your personal information with honesty and trust with others, you will not be able to build good relationships. And you will be missing out on opportunities to enjoy life as strong relationships are a source of great happiness.

When a discussion leads to revealing yourself, do you divert the discussion to another topic? Does it happen often? If yes, see if it is coming in the way of building relationships.

Till you complete reading this book, keep an open mind and put on your logical thinking hat. Some of the ideas may be completely contradictory to your own. Don't go by your emotions, evaluate them objectively. Accept them only after a thorough analysis.

Being open does not mean that you have to reveal the mistakes you have committed or fantasies you have. Some of the thoughts or events that you experienced need not be revealed, even to the closest friend. You have the right to keep them as your secrets forever.

## Step 7

### Realize You are Alone.

In this world, you are alone as far as your feelings and thoughts are concerned. It is romantic to feel that we can share our feelings 100% with other people. But in reality, your feelings are yours.

Throughout our lives, we want to influence others for our well-being, and others also want to influence us. We develop a relationship of dependence, which is vital to our physical survival. But in this process, we become dependent on psychological well-being too. It is especially true with your close people such as spouse, siblings, parents, friends, colleagues, etc. But, irrespective of the type of relationship you have, many times you have to battle your emotional wars alone. It is futile to expect another person to be there with you all the time for the emotional battles. So, we should accept the fact that even in a highly romantic relationship or lovable relationship you will feel alone sometimes. And it is the same with others. Knowing this fact, you should practice enjoying being alone physically as well as emotionally.

My experience of many years of marriage, and the experience of psychological counseling that I provided to the public for many years has helped me realize that our feelings or emotions are unique to ourselves. We ALONE can feel the way we feel, and no one else can feel it the same way. But others can help us change our feelings. There will be times when you feel completely alone, and you should learn to accept it and stay happy.

So, how do we go about living happily? Turn to the next chapter.

---***---

# Chapter #3
# A Roadmap to Happiness

You already know what makes you happy. Don't you? You keep experiencing it now and then. The challenge is to experience happiness more often. If I ask you, how can you have happiness more often? A typical response could be having more of those situations that give you happiness. But you and I know very well that it is just wishful thinking and is completely impractical. So, the practical approach is to gain control over our emotions and learn to experience happiness, to the extent possible, in every situation.

To begin with, internalizing the 7 steps of the last chapter is essential to leading a happy life. You need to evaluate your actions as well as reactions, with those ideas in mind. If you have agreed with **Step #3 (Being happy is the ultimate purpose of life)** "Living happily" should become your ultimate goal. It should be your CONSCIOUS decision.

***You should aim to maximize your happy moments at the expense of momentary ego-satisfying gains.***

For example, let us say you are stuck in a traffic jam. A typical immediate reaction would be anger coupled with an urge to curse others. If you fall prey to this impulse, you will be adding unhappy moments to your life. If you are ***"Selfishk"***, you would use that time positively and effectively to add happiness moments. You will then think about available options such as listening to music, having a meaningful conversation with co-passengers, or thinking about something else that would add value.

Let me diverge a little here to explain the word "***S-e-l-f-i-s-h-k***". [See the next page]

## *Selfishk*

/ˈselfɪʃk/
Adjective

I am introducing this word to mean:

- *"Loving oneself without causing hurt to others"*
- *"Taking care of self, but not at the expense of others"*
- *"Focusing on self-interests without ignoring responsibilities"*

This word is made of two words from two different languages. It is the combination of the word "***Self***" from the English language, and the word "***Ishk***" from Hindi whose meaning is **'love'**.

***Selfishk*** = **Self** + ***Ishk***

So "***Self+Ishk***" means **'Self Love'**, without the negative feelings associated with the word selfish. [Thanks to my friend "***Ravi Patruni***" for inventing this word on my request]

While discussing this word, one of my brothers told me about Ayn Rand and her books. Her book "The Virtue of Selfishness", a collection of essays, talks elaborately about the negative connotation of the word "Selfish".

## Importance of the Present Moment

The key to happiness lies in the PRESENT moment. You should always focus on the PRESENT moment and validate how it is contributing to your happiness. Why focus on the PRESENT? Because that is ***the only time you LIVE***. It sounds cliché, right? But it is a fact. All that we have to do is to master this moment.

For example, if you feel you are wasting your PRESENT time by reading this book, and you feel you can spend this time in a better way somewhere else, you should immediately put this book aside and leave. But if you feel this investment of time can lead to MORE happy moments later in life, continue reading happily.

Be conscious of what is happening to you at every moment - to your body, to your emotions, to your feelings. It is very difficult to have this control. It needs a good amount of practice. For now, just try telling yourself to monitor your feelings every moment. Remind yourself every time to evaluate if your behavior and thinking at that moment are adding happiness moments to your life or not.

Living in the Present does not mean ignoring the Past or the Future. It is okay to recollect Past events, and it is okay and necessary to think about Future events. What you should focus is on your current feelings during that process of thinking. Let us say, you remember an event when a friend misbehaved with you, and it hurt you very badly at that time. If that same person happens to meet you now, you might recollect past events and experience the same feelings again. You might feel anger, and resentment even if this person behaves well at this moment. At this very moment, if you remember your goal, you can choose to have happy moments added instead of negative feelings.

Recollect **Step #4 (The root cause of your unhappiness is your mind)**. You will agree with me that most of the time the PRESENT moment will be pleasant. Your unhappiness at any point in time is, almost always, due to the PAST events or the FUTURE.

It does not matter HOW MANY years you live. But what matters is HOW YOU LIVE. So, choose to live happily, and live in such a way that you enjoy your PRESENT moment even while thinking about the Past or the Future.

## Why Is It Difficult to Be Happy in Every Moment?

Let us look at why it is difficult to be happy in every moment. It is because each situation is very different as we have many things to take care of. Most of us have family responsibilities. I guess you struggle the same way as I struggle to take care of them. If you were a hermit the challenges would be very few. The situations we face have consequences lasting from a very short time to a long time. Let us look at some of these situations and see how we can handle them in a better way. For the sake of our discussion, let us categorize the situations based on the impact time or length of consequences.

### Ephemeral:

Take the example of the traffic jam we discussed above. If the delay due to the traffic jam is not going to cause any major issues, the consequence is ephemeral. So, it does not make any sense to get upset. Choose an alternative reaction that can add value or happiness moments.

Let us take another example, say you are working on your computer or reading a book, and your loved one wants to discuss something. And if this intrusion causes only a minor disturbance i.e., the consequence has a limited time, there is no need to get upset. You get upset if you consider the other work as low value. Remember **Step #5? (No work is inferior. Enjoy every task you do. And do it to your best).** So, again choose the reaction that can add more moments of happiness.

**Short Time:**

Continuing with the previous example, let us say there is a pattern in the behavior of your loved one that disturbs you EVERY TIME you are doing something. As this behavior has consequences beyond the current situation, you will have to take an appropriate action that works in controlling the other person's behavior. It can be shouting angrily, looking sternly, pleading, or reasoning out.  But if you choose an aggressive reaction, it might result in your heart beating faster and you feeling wretched. So, you need to learn to show aggressiveness without the accompanying emotional and physical reactions.

Let us take another example. Say, you have to attend a meeting on time. You are ready, and you have just enough time to have your breakfast and leave.  Just then you spilled a drink on your pants. You may get irritated with yourself and start worrying about attending the meeting on time. Or you can choose to stay calm and think about the options available. You have 2 options here. You can skip your breakfast and use the available time to change your dress, or you can ask for the meeting to be postponed.

**Long Time:**

Some situations have a long-term impact such as the loss of a job, a divorce, or death of a loved one. In these situations, the future appears very bleak, and we find ourselves to be alone. You are lucky if you find support from your family and friends. Despite this, you might feel that no one understands your feelings correctly. It is okay to feel sad, but it is important to remember **Step #7 (Realize you are alone).** By nature, each one of us is alone. We cannot expect others to understand our feelings and emotions correctly. With this realization, we should learn to be comfortable with ourselves as well as our loneliness.

Let us say you lost your job. It will have implications for your finances as well as for your self-esteem. The immediate feeling could be that of losing respect in society. And due to financial loss, you might have to cut down or lower your lifestyle. Even if you have the means to live, this fact of living at a lower standard might bother you. We have instances of people going to the extent of committing suicide due to this loss of face. I have personally seen many people struggle to hide the fact that they were jobless and that they were forced to lower their lifestyle. Internalizing **Step #6 (Be open. Let others know you)** will help you grounded. If you develop the attitude of being okay with everyone knowing you as you are, it will work as a shock absorber. Finally, remember Step **#2 (Nature demands that we live our full life, and allow our species to continue).** Nothing more nothing less. All other things are secondary. As long as you have the basic minimum means to survive, there is no need to worry. In case you have to work, if you agree with **Step #5 (No work is inferior. Enjoy every task you do. And do it to your best)**, you will find work that can give you enough money for your survival.

As we discussed earlier, the reason for your current unhappiness lies in either PAST or FUTURE. Look at children and look at other living beings. We realize that they are always in bliss, content with what they have. Reason: they always live in the PRESENT. Whenever you feel unhappy, look at the present moment (that particular second), I bet it will always be neutral if not pleasant. Remember **Step #3 (Being happy is the purpose of life)** - our goal is to stay happy, so we should focus on accumulating maximum happy moments. It is not worth spoiling the Present moment for the Past or Future. Does it mean that we can be apathetic to the goings-on in this world, just to accumulate happy moments?

## Can You Be Apathetic?

Can you be apathetic to activities that are happening around you? Let us say, two people are fighting and there is a chance you can pacify them. But if you are involved, you might lose your happiness. If you just ignore or be apathetic you might retain your calm. Is that the way we should live? Maybe yes!

Let us say that one of the people involved is your loved one. Will your answer be the same? Absolutely not. You have to learn to differentiate one situation from the other. And you should train yourself to think and choose the right action. And if you have mastered the art of staying happy, you can intervene without losing your calm, or for that matter, you can intervene happily.

Let me give a real-life example. A few years back, precisely on 23-Sept-2014, a boy fell accidentally into the enclosure of a Tiger at Delhi Zoo. The Tiger stared at him confused for almost 15 minutes. Later the Tiger pounced on him and killed him. All that the visitors at the zoo could do was shout, pelt stones, etc., but could not rescue him. If you were one of the spectators there, what would you have done in that situation? I asked myself the same question. I realized that I would not have done anything different than others.

But, if it were my daughter who fell into the Tiger enclosure, I would have jumped into the enclosure without any hesitation. I would not have even thought about the consequences at that time. The first reaction is to be by her side to protect her. It is a natural reaction of every living thing to protect its offspring. Recollect **Step #2 (Nature demands that we live our full life and allow our species to continue)** - it is at play. Even though this action harms me physically, it would give me an immense sense of satisfaction even if I were to die in that process.

So, the next question is, "*How do we decide what is the right action?*" You must test your actions with a simple rule: ***Whatever actions you intend to take if everyone on this planet follows it, it should result in an overall positive feeling.***

Going by **Step #1 (All living creatures are equal)**, you should realize that you are neither superior nor inferior to anyone. You should keep that in mind while contemplating the actions you want to undertake. You should imagine that whatever actions you take everyone else in this world also can take them. Remember this Golden rule:

### Golden Rule for Action

***For any action, check if EVERYONE does what you are going to do, is it good or bad?***

*Use this test every time you are in a dilemma. I am sure it will provide you the direction. Let me illustrate this with a small story. Once upon a time in India, a King wanted to test the honesty of his people. So, he asked everyone to bring a mug of milk to the palace and pour it into a container. He announced clearly that no one would be checking their mugs. All the citizens complied with that request. The next day, when the King checked the container, to his surprise he found the entire container filled with water. You can guess what happened there. Every person thought his mug of water would go unnoticed in the big container of milk! If they applied the "Golden Rule for Action", they could have acted differently.*

There will be situations when you feel sad, angry, etc. It is okay to feel that as long as it is not debilitating you. See what Dr. Happiness says about happiness.

A famous psychologist Dr. Ed Diener, who is also known as Dr. Happiness, used the term Subjective Well Being (SWB) to measure happiness levels. As per him,

> *"A person is said to have high Subjective Well-Being (SWB) if she or he experiences life satisfaction and frequent joy, and only infrequently experiences unpleasant emotions such as sadness and anger."*

Let us look at now, how we can actively experience happiness and increase our SWB (Subjective Well-Being). It is simple - ***Just take charge of the PRESENT moment***. No need to go back in life and change events, or no need to hop onto a time machine to set the Future perfect. There are many books written to drive home this point - "Live in the Present Moment".

## Take Charge of the Present Moment

You need to take charge of the Present moment to meet your goal. Even though it is a simple proposition, it takes a lot of practice to gain that control. It requires control over your thoughts, emotions, and overall - your mind.

You might have heard people say that "Life is full of suffering and pain". It is NOT correct. ***Life is full of joy and sharing.*** Think about it from nature's perspective. Look at the plants and animals. Look at nature. Look at it from the perspective of a child. The entire nature is amazing, mesmerizing, entertaining, and awe-inspiring. It is fun to be born and alive. Yes, during one's life, an individual faces a few physical challenges in the form of diseases, old age, and death. But, for a large percentage of people in this world, it is a very small price to pay. [For a very few people with serious physical disabilities life can become very challenging and traumatic. Even in those conditions also we have seen great personalities bloom- Stephen Hawking is one of them]. As far as the psychological challenges are concerned, they are man-made. All that you have been reading in this book is about how to face those challenges and overcome them. By this time, you might have realized how important the 7 steps are. They are the building blocks. Internalizing them is essential for happiness. Discuss those steps with others. Brainstorm. Set aside some time for each step - think, analyze, internalize.

**To take charge of the present moment, there are two things that you should learn:**

1. **Choose Action over Rumination**
2. **Be Child-like**

### 1. Choose Action Over Rumination:

Taking charge of the present moment means thinking and choosing the right way to react. What you do in the present moment is what adds up to the way you have lived. Every situation demands that you CHOOSE the response. Whatever is the response, it is your CHOICE. Unfortunately, many of our responses are automatic, and impulsive i.e., they are not under our control. It is the result of our CONDITIONING. The challenge is to overcome that and be a free person. It will take many months and years to reach that stage. You will learn the technique to de-condition yourself and to become free, in the next chapters.

Do you spend your present time thinking about past or future events again and again?

If you said yes, then you are ruminating. The events you ruminate about can be positive or negative. But instead of generating new experiences or living in the present, you end up living in the past or future. The positive events might help you add happy moments for now. But if you become dependent on the rumination of those events for your happiness, it is an alert for you to wake up. On the other hand, ruminating about negative events leads to worry and anxiety.

So, watch out for rumination and put a stop to it as it cannot change anything. Think about what you can do now to add value to your situation. Let us say, a loved one is sick and is being treated by a qualified doctor. You might be overwhelmed with the thoughts of something going wrong. If you keep thinking about that negative outcome again and again, it does not change the situation on the ground. You need to evaluate what you can do best in that situation and take the required action. It could be alleviating the pain by making the sick person physically comfortable, boosting that person's mood with some wise comments, or taking the opinion of other experts about the situation. Whatever it is, act. Because it can only improve the situation.

**2. Be Child-like:**

The key to happiness is living in the moment with full awareness. By the way, I am not going to propose any lofty theories or philosophical discussions about *living, the moment,* or *awareness*. It is simple, to enjoy the moment, be a Child [For more information, refer to the Internet for Eric Berne's "Ego States"] whenever you can. Be an Adult if the situation demands you to think and decide. Being aware means being in the know of the reality at that moment, being able to assess the situation realistically, being able to look at the options, and being able to choose the appropriate option based on the situation.

As we grow up, many of us lose the Child in us. The typical Child in us is playful, wants to have fun, and enjoys doing things for the sake of doing - in short, lives carefree in that moment. Grab these moments. Spend time doing whatever you like without worrying about the effectiveness. Take a walk, listen to music, paint a picture, dance to a tune, play a game with your significant others, have a chat with friends or close family members, cook a dish, wash your car, practice whatever you always wanted to, just look around and enjoy watching things as they are, or just do nothing. [Interestingly, religious ceremonies, spiritual events, and rituals allow you to be a Child. They incorporate Child-like activities such as singing, and dancing into their routines. Many elderly people shed their inhibitions and join others to take part in these rituals. You will find people experiencing ecstasy and start crying or laughing without being self-conscious.] Recollect **Step #3 (Being happy is the purpose of life)**, your goal should be adding as many moments of this nature as possible to your life.

Wait a second!...
When was the last time you enjoyed like a Child?

*It is time you bring your Child out!*

You might say, "Oh! Okay, all that you said about living in the moment and being a Child is great. But that is where the struggle is!". I fully agree with you. Unfortunately, we have been taught to associate our happiness with outside events. When you long for something and you get it, say a fancy car, you feel high. You might have noticed that the joy and happiness of owning that thing lasts for a short period only. And to get the same level of happiness you will have to get more and more of it. And the object that gave you joy may not give the same joy to others. Interestingly, it may not give the same joy to you in a different situation. Why is the experience different? It is due to your ***mindset*** at that particular moment! The external thing is the same, but how you perceived, or others perceived made the difference. It is your mind that interprets it in different ways. If you recollect some of the examples that I gave in the earlier chapters, your mindset decides your emotions of happiness, sadness, etc. Your emotions are the result of your thinking and your upbringing. You can always learn to think in a positive way and become emotionally strong. You must realize that the feeling of happiness is the result of your ***mindset,*** and it is ***internal to you***. The good thing about it being internal is that you can have control over it. For that matter...

> ***...Your MINDSET is the only thing that can be fully controlled by you with effort and practice.***

It is not the same with external factors. You cannot always control the external things fully. But with practice, you can gain control over your mindset i.e., your emotions and attitude, and find happiness in everything you do.

Let us now look at the 3 most common ways people get their happiness and see how they become victims. I call them 3 traps as they force you into a rat race, and many times they can cause unhappiness too.

## The 3 Traps

Almost all of us are brainwashed to focus on success and achievements from a very young age. We have been rewarded and punished accordingly. In simple words, we have been CONDITIONED to feel happy only when there was a success. This conditioning has led us to experience happiness in certain situations only. All these situations can be classified into 3 broad categories:

1. Recognition/Acceptance
2. Wealth
3. Power

### 1. Recognition/Acceptance:

Are you worried about your social status? Are you worried about the likes you get on social media? Are you worried about your looks? In general, are you worried about what others think about you? If you say yes to any one of them, then you are looking for others' acceptance of you.

Check yourself with these other questions. Do you put extra effort into pleasing someone? Do you get overly elated when someone praises you? If you said yes, it might be an indication that you give greater value to others' evaluations of you. You might be working knowingly or unknowingly to seek their recognition/acceptance. Many young people have lost their lives while trying to outdo others or get others' recognition. The case in point is that of Internet trends - the "Challenges" on social media. A few lost their lives, and many got permanently disabled while taking up the challenges and recording them. To name a few - Blue Whale Challenge, Subway surfing, Cinnamon Challenge, Punch 4 Punch.

If you have not mastered the art of happiness, you might be looking forward to others' recognition/approval of your work for your happiness. Society, whether it is a corporate world or a non-corporate world, uses this phenomenon to control you. Many people succumb to this trap and spend their whole time and effort to garner recognition. When this recognition is not forthcoming, they feel dejected and get depressed. Important people in your life can use this effectively to control your behavior by withholding appreciation. Look into yourself and find your approval-seeking urges. Remember **Step #6 (Be open. Let others know you).** Be yourself. You are unique in this world. Accept whatever the way you are. But be open to criticism, and if there is something that you can do to improve your personality, embrace it. Sometimes others may not see your point of view, and you get frustrated. Remember **Step #7 (Realize you are alone)**, it is not possible for anyone in this world to fully understand you as you feel. It is okay to feel lonely. It is natural. Recognize that fact and accept being alone.

**2. Wealth:**

This is a well-known reason to be happy. Yes, money is required for our survival and comfort, and we should make every effort to earn it. Here again, we have been conditioned to feel good and happy only when we can buy an expensive toy - say a car, a house, an expensive watch, etc. I am sure you might have realized that the happiness of owning something expensive does not last long. As soon as a better version of the same comes, it loses value in terms of giving you happiness. It is okay to buy happiness this way, as long as you are not getting into debt or making your life miserable. But many people go out of their way to work single-mindedly on owning these and becoming rich. In that process, many of them miss out on the opportunities of accumulating happy moments. In some cases, it becomes too late for them to realize this.

If you agree with **Step #3 (Being happy is the purpose of life)**, you should focus on accumulating happy moments. But money is important for survival. So, you should learn to survive with the bare minimum of money and make enough investments to provide for that in the long run. Without enough money, life becomes very difficult, and staying happy becomes a tough challenge.

### 3. Power:

This is akin to intoxication. Having control over the resources helps you live comfortably. But many people love having this control over the resources (including people) just for the sake of having power. History is replete with innumerable stories of greed for power, and the damage it has done to the individual as well as to humanity as a whole. You will find the power structure in every place - in the family, in an organization, in a community, etc. People make many sacrifices to gain the power they are interested in. For each of them, based on the situation they are in, the ultimate power they want will be different. In a private company, it could be reaching the position of CEO; in a non-profit or religious or spiritual organization it could be the overall head; in a country, it could be President or Prime Minister, etc. Some crave the position for monetary benefit, and some for the sake of power itself. And achieving that gives them happiness. In a typical corporate world, people work very hard to get promotions at the expense of their personal life. In that process, they get highly stressed out and struggle to maintain a proper work-life balance. As I said earlier, some people go to any extent to grab the power as they get the kick out of it. So, you, as an individual, should decide how much to sacrifice for the sake of power, so that you can maximize your happy moments. Remember the "Golden Rule for Action" and decide what is right for you.

Am I saying, "Do not go after recognition, wealth, and/or power"? No, definitely not! I am asking you to pay attention to the sacrifices you are making to get them. In all the 3 cases, your happiness is dependent on external factors, comparisons with other people, etc. And you are aware that you may lose all or some of them at any point in the future. If you have built your happiness world on them, this awareness, in turn, will create the fear of losing them. This fear will cause unhappiness and make you expend more effort to protect them from falling apart. That is the reason I am calling them traps.

As your goal is to achieve happiness, you should focus on staying happy without depending on external factors. Happiness is internal to you. It is all about how you perceive the goings-on. As we discussed above, it needs control over how you think and choose to react. If you can enjoy every moment and not get affected by the negative results, you can pursue all the 3 things stated above while enjoying the journey. For that, you need to gain control over your emotions first. ***You should reach a stage where you do not need a reason to be happy***. You should learn to stay calm/be at peace/feel joy and live in the moment.

Once again remember **Step #3 (Being happy is the purpose of life)** - any person who lived his life happily, without causing unhappiness to others, had served his purpose. It does not matter whether that person is a laborer, a janitor, a teacher, a businessman, a scientist, or a politician.

---***---

# Chapter #4
# Break the 3 Boulders

There are many books on happiness - self-help, spiritual, psychological. There are many organizations, societies, and sects that are actively involved in teaching happiness. There is abundant literature explaining the dos & don'ts of finding happiness. In the process of advocating the path to happiness, many an organization communicated some wrong ideas adding to the conundrum. In this chapter, let us actively look at some key Myths and try to bust them.

## Myth #1

### Money Cannot Buy Happiness!

You might have heard this many times. This is incorrect. Money is very important for your existence and well-being. If you are a family man like me, it is absolutely necessary to have a good amount of money. If you have lots of money, it makes it easy to live happily. You need money unless you have abandoned your family, become an ascetic, and joined an ashram that provides free shelter and food. I repeat,

***"Money makes it easy to live happily."***

You should use the money to BUY happiness. This is contrary to many sages who say money cannot buy happiness. Let me give an example. Let us say, you need to attend an important meeting outstation the next day. You have planned to take an overnight bus. But, at your home, a close family member is unwell, and the person wants you to be around during the night. If you have money, you can take an early morning flight. That way you can take care of your loved one, and you can keep up with your appointments too. Now, you as well as your family members are happy. How did you get this Happiness? You BOUGHT that with money. This does not mean you need to spend all the money for happiness in the present moment. You must make provisions for your future happiness too. That is the balance you need to strike. Once you learn how to be happy, the amount of money you need for your happiness diminishes. It can lead to having extra money on your hands. And you may use that to make more money.

The other good thing about money is, ***it is a great motivator***. To earn more money, you need to contribute more value. Having more money is a privilege. If you wish so, you can utilize the extra money to help many others become happy.

So, why do some people say, "Money is a bad thing"? Because it can lead to unhappiness if you go after it with single-minded devotion at the expense of all other things in life. If you keep the goal of being happy as your top priority, you can enjoy the game of making money by appropriately allocating your time. So, go after it and make more money. The money in the hands of good people like you is good for society. Extending it further, you can spend money to make many people happy if you intend to. In this context, we should remember one person - **Charles "Chuck" Feeney**[1] - a champion of "Giving While Living". Since 1982, throughout his life, he has donated more than $8 billion anonymously.

On the other hand, not having enough money can seriously affect your happiness. It leads to great stress as simple demands of living cannot be met easily. In my experience as a Psychological Counselor, I have seen stress due to financial problems to be the most challenging of all problems. People who get into debt, or whose expenses are much higher than their incomes are most vulnerable to depression. So, it is prudent to keep one's living expenses to the bare minimum.

## Myth #2

### Making Others Happy Gives You the Best Happiness!

Do you subscribe to this idea? Some gurus go to the extent of saying that your "**purpose of life**" is to make others happy, and only that gives you true/real happiness. Many scriptures appear to be advocating that you must live for the sake of others. On the face of it, these principles appear to be good when you look at them from others' perspective i.e., society's perspective. But in reality, it can lead to exploitation by cunning individuals or organizations.

Think about it! Let us say somehow, I convinced you that you can get real happiness only by making others happy. Imagine you subscribed to this idea wholeheartedly. Now, if I were a cunning individual, I could ask you to make me happy at the expense of your well-being, and you end up being a servile individual. Thus, you get into the trap of serving people and ignoring your interests. And you may end up becoming a bondservant to other people. Many pseudo-gurus have used this technique to commit innumerable atrocities on innocent people.

But we know that we do get happiness by making others happy. You agree with me, right? Then what are we discussing here? That is the catch. ***"Making others happy" is a shortcut to immediate happiness.*** It is akin to getting a kick out of a drink or indulging in physical pleasure. The act of making others happy by giving alms or helping them in an activity makes us feel a little superior; and boosts our self-esteem. If you are feeling low, and if you have not mastered the art of staying happy, you can indulge in this pastime. It is definitely NOT the best kind of happiness; it is a short-term solution until you gain full control over your happiness.

*A person who mastered the art of being happy may end up spending more time making others happy.*

But the converse may not be the right thing for you i.e., getting happiness only by making others happy.

For a minute, let us imagine this is the only way you get happiness i.e., by making others happy. Further, imagine everyone else is already happy. What will happen to your happiness? Mull over this thought for a while.

- You get happiness only when you give alms to poor people, but no one needs your alms. What will happen to your happiness?
- You get happiness by helping disabled people cross the road. But, let us say, there are no disabled persons, and no one needs others' help. What will happen to your happiness?

I hope you get my point of view.

***When your happiness is DEPENDENT on others, you are in trouble.***

In certain neurotic cases, people end up wishing that others become dependent on them so that they (the neurotic persons) get their happiness.

Many studies indicate that helping others is the major contributor to happiness. The reason for this is that a greater percentage of people find it so. On a normal curve i.e., the Bell curve (see the picture) of happy people, the majority gets more satisfaction through that behavior.

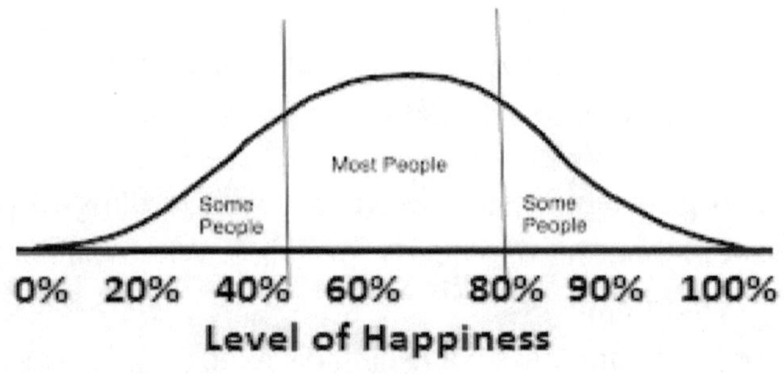


Note: It is representative. The % are NOT accurate.

The outliers, on the rightmost, are the people who mastered the art of happiness. Their happiness is purely internal; it is not dependent on external factors. Many of the happiness studies conducted by Psychologists are based on surveys/interviews of people. So, naturally, the ideas communicated belong to the MOST of the people, which turns out to be people whose level of happiness is less than the peak level of happiness.

## Myth #3

### Seeking Pleasures Leads You Away from the Path of Happiness!

Not necessarily. Pleasure-seeking is good for you. It can add to your happiness. It becomes a problem when you become dependent on them, or your actions hurt you or others. Enjoy life's pleasures without hurting anyone. For example, I love watching Kung Fu movies. I enjoy watching them again and again. Nothing wrong with that. If for any reason, I am not allowed to watch them, and I start feeling unhappy then it becomes a problem.

***The pursuit of pleasure,***
***self-indulgence in sensual pleasures,***
***in short ethical Hedonism***
***is welcome.***

Enjoy your favorite food, drink, exercise, game, etc. Be ***selfishk***. Enjoy all bodily pleasures without guilt as long as you are not hurting yourself or others. A glass of wine or your favorite drink every day may give you immense pleasure. But if you ignore your health, spend all your money, or ignore your family responsibilities, it may hurt you more than the pleasure you get. To maximize your happiness, you should learn to be happy now, and learn to invest for happiness in the future.

Some of the religious teachers, Gurus encourage an ascetic life to gain happiness. Abstinence, renunciation, and teetotalism are some of the things they advocate. The mere adherence to them without really having inner peace will be counterproductive. But, ***leading a life of simple means, experiencing and enduring pain, can help you reduce the threshold of happiness.*** These rigors of practice may help the individual reduce his/her dependence on those pleasures for his happiness.

Real happiness is the feeling that you have inside. The inner feeling of calm, joy, and bliss is what happiness stands for. To be happy, you need not always have to have pleasurable experiences, even in pain, you can find happiness. Does it make any sense? Pain and happiness? Think for a moment. Can you recollect situations where you were in immense pain, but felt happy? If you said "Yes", you could skip the following examples, otherwise read them through.

- A child who plays outdoors might get hurt and experience pain.
- A Martial artist goes through rigorous pain to strengthen his mind and body.

But in both cases, they love to do what they do, and it makes them happy. And keep in mind that you can be happy even when you are in pain. In gist, seeking happiness in pleasurable things is not necessarily a bad thing as long as you are in control.

--***--

# Chapter #5
## Living Your Own Life

Are you overwhelmed with all that we have discussed so far? The concepts are simple, and I hope you find them rational and logical. You might have come across these ideas sometime or other. All these have been documented in many different ways by our forefathers i.e., great thinkers, philosophers, religious leaders, etc. Despite its wide availability, many of us could not learn and adapt them to life. Knowing is one thing and applying it is another. As my hero, Bruce Lee said:

> ***"Knowing is not enough, we must apply.***
> ***Willing is not enough, we must do."***

Applying knowledge takes a lot of practice and patience. So, keep reminding yourself about the 7 steps that we have discussed. That is the blueprint for evaluating your actions. At this point, you may not agree 100% with each of the steps. But

go back and check again periodically to see to what extent you agree with them. Moving to the next step in that ladder requires gaining an insight into the earlier step(s).

|  |
|---|
| Step #1: **All living beings - humans, animals, plants, including insects - are equal.**<br>Okay! What next? |
| Step #2: **Nature demands that we live our full life, and allow our species to continue.**<br>How do I live? |
| Step #3: **Being happy is the ultimate purpose of life.**<br>How can I be happy? |
| Step #4: **Realize that the root cause of your unhappiness is your mind.**<br>What actions should I undertake? |
| Step #5: **No work is inferior. Enjoy every task you do. And do it to your best.**<br>What do people think about my work? |
| Step #6: **Be Open. Let others know you.**<br>Do people accept me? |
| Step #7: **Realize you are alone.**<br>Start enjoying solitude! |

The challenge is now applying this knowledge to our daily lives.

We must develop control over our minds to remind ourselves of this knowledge and act accordingly. If we were to live alone in a secluded place, we would have to fight just against our minds. But as we live in a society, we need to take on others' minds too. So, the challenges of daily living can be segregated into two categories:

The TWO main challenges of daily living are:

1. Living your own life
2. Getting along with others

## Living Your Own Life

Imagine you are healthy and all alone in a Japanese hotel "The Henn-na, or Strange Hotel" - the world's first hotel with all-Robot staff. Imagine you have abundant money so you can afford the services of this hotel. During your entire stay, all your material needs such as food, cosmetics, laundry services, etc. are met by robots, and you won't see any human beings. Imagine you're staying there for 365 days i.e. for a whole year. Further imagine that there is no TV, no newspaper, no mobile or no communication with others. Will you be able to spend every day happily?

Forget about happiness, just living there for 365 days in the above-specified conditions needs strong determination and perseverance. For sure, you will go mad. If this were a 'challenge', and you could go back to society after 365 days to narrate your story, maybe you can somehow pull along. Imagine that you will forget everything that happens in this hotel, and you are not allowed to document anything. How do you spend every minute of your 365 days? Take a minute and reflect!

In the first few days, you might like the novelty and you might enjoy the hospitality of the Robots. You might enjoy the fact that you need not do any work and you have slaves i.e. Robots doing all the work for you.

What will happen after a week or a few weeks?

## Spending Time Meaningfully

You will get bored, and frustrated! You might have tried everything in the world to keep yourself busy so far. By this time, you might have gone through in your mind all the events that have passed in your life, not just once, but many times over. But now, you will find it difficult, and more difficult to SPEND time as days go by. **"How to structure your time and spend every minute available?"**, becomes the biggest challenge. In this situation, you will start thinking about the purpose of your life, the meaning of your life, and in general why you were born in this big cosmic world. So many questions will arise in your mind. And despite having every material thing that you need and provided to you at your beckoning, it might lead to depression and suicidal tendencies. [Note: If you are left in a jungle to fend for yourself, it would be a little different. For some time, the challenge of surviving will keep you engaged.]

> "***How to spend the time given to us by life***"- is the greatest challenge for every one of us.

Life is all about spending the time we have. So, people get attracted to things that help them spend time without a serious effort of thinking. That is the reason why people who engage you and entertain you such as sports people and film personalities get paid handsomely. Similarly, when the so-called gurus or spiritual leaders ask people to "Surrender" by promising salvation or solutions for individuals' problems, people love it. It takes away the great burden of thinking about spending time. So, many people lovingly hold onto rituals that might appear meaningless to others. It gives them an anchor to get through their life.

[This was the core concept of the famous Psychiatrist Dr. Viktor E. Frankel's theory of "Logotherapy". It is focused on the meaning of human existence as well as on man's search for such a meaning.]

Why do you get bored in the above situation? Your immediate response could be that it was all routine. Everything you asked for has been attended to, and you have nothing much to do except to eat, wander, and sleep. As mentioned above, if you were asked to fend for yourself, you would have had a variety of things to do. It could have given you the required stimulation for you to act and get involved in an activity. In the absence of a physical challenge, the challenges that involve just your mind would also help you engage. So, to get over boredom, and to get excited, we look for physical or psychological stimulation. Once we get used to stimulation, we lose the excitement part and look for higher levels of stimulation or different forms of it.

Take for example the fact that you get thrills by going on rides in an amusement park. If you go on the same ride multiple times, you will feel less and less of the adrenalin-pumping experience. To get the same level of *high* as you got on the first ride, you will look forward to the scarier, more difficult ride. It is the same case with day-to-day activities. We get bored with our car, our household items, our work, or our relationships, and look forward to something different. This is the reason we have the saying "Variety is the spice of life". Many people accept it as *the way to live.* **But it is an indication that you have become *dependent* on external factors for your excitement.** Your mind becomes sort of slave to them, will be longing for more and more of the stimulation. We need to realize that the feeling of excitement is internal to us. For that matter, all emotions we experience are internal to us. We can learn to gain control over them with the right mindset and practice.

One of the ways is to have a Child-like mindset to enjoy the small things of everyday life.  A child gets excited about the simple things around him and enjoys playing with them. As mentioned in an earlier chapter, develop a Child-like attitude. Notice the surroundings, be curious, appreciate the beauty of the world, and get immersed in it. You should reach the stage where you can enjoy being alone and not doing anything. You might say, there are many people already doing that lazing around, what is the difference? The difference is that of control. The lazy guy can do that ONLY, but you have the choice. Your actions are not controlled by external factors. You can choose to do what you want, and one of them is being alone and doing nothing. For outsiders, the external behavior of the lazy person and yours appear the same, oblivious to the fact of the enormous control you have.

That is what is meant by the Zen saying:

> *"Before enlightenment,*
>
> *chop wood, carry water.*
>
> *After enlightenment,*
>
> *chop wood, carry water."*
>
> ***- Zen saying***

Unfortunately, in this highly connected world with the mobile phone and the Internet, people are losing the capacity to "do nothing". Everyone these days is always "on" on social media such as Facebook, WhatsApp, and Instagram, playing video games, or always listening to music by cutting off the external world. They are becoming addicted to these ways of spending time, and have to go through de-addiction programs such as "social media detox", "Digital detox" etc. See if you are one of them, and plan ways to minimize such dependency.

Now, let us come back to our "Henn-na" hotel and see what can happen with you there.

## Social Relationships

As you continue to live in this "Henn-na" hotel, you will start interacting more with the robots. Luckily for you, some of the robots are made to look like humans. You will start giving it a name, a personality. Let us say, all the robots are made to look like just machines i.e. no human features are given to them. You might find it difficult to treat them as humans. But eventually, over some time, you will start interacting with them as if they are humans. Have you seen the movie "Castaway"? In that, the "volleyball" becomes "Wilson", a friend to the hero. The hero keeps communicating with "it" as if it is human. An inanimate thing, unlike a robot, which does not even move on its own becomes a companion in these extreme conditions. If you were to find a living thing such as a lizard, cockroach, or rat, I am sure you would love to see them more and more. And for all you know you might make it a pet. You will start showing and expressing all your emotions towards that pet. This interaction will mostly take care of your problem of spending time as well as your need for social contact. You might have heard about people leaving huge wealth behind for their pets. This is the reason for that. The pets fulfill their need for social interactions as well as the problem of spending time.

**To live your own life,**
**you need to take care of the following:**

- **Spending the available time effectively**
- **Having social interactions**

Not having anything to do, and not having social relationships is a serious problem. If someone struggles to earn a living every day is not that bad, if he can make ends meet. If this guy had a family that was waiting for him at home, he would be the happiest. This is what intrigued the researchers of "Positive Psychology", when they found the 'rickshaw-wallahs' of Kolkata, India, experiencing happiness despite the hard life. They were determined to find out how a person could be happy in those extremely poor conditions - such as living day-to-day without sufficient food, living in a shanty without drainage or toilets, and surrounded by filth, etc. The reason for the 'rickshaw-wallahs' happiness is the 'needs' of their circumstances. The circumstances have given these persons both above, "a meaningful way to spend time" and "a caring family for social interactions".

In some cases (maybe in many cases) having just a pet at home to go back to motivates people to live. Interestingly people love pets more than their close family members. The main reason is that pets give you unconditional love. In human relationships receiving unconditional love is rare as every human generally looks for reciprocity.

--***--

# Chapter #6
# Getting Along with Others

It has been proved beyond doubt that we all need social interactions to grow from a newborn baby to an adult. We need at least one person, real or imaginary, for our survival. You can understand that from the "Henn-na" mental exercise too that we need social relationships for our survival. Even when a person works alone in a spaceship or is ready to go to Mars on a no-return mission, they take it up for the challenge and for the research that helps others. There is always a reason that is tied to another human being. It could be helping, taking care of the other; or it could be vengeance, jealousy; or it could be trying to get another person's attention by proving oneself, etc.

It is very clear that to continue our life we have to interact with others. The number of interactions gets multiplied with time as well as with the number of people. This becomes a major challenge as we need to handle our emotions and actions based on others' emotions and actions. And they keep changing and the variety of interactions can be infinite.

So, the question is, how can we handle all this?

## Your Conditioning

This is the same problem your parents had, your teachers had, and your elders had with you as a kid. They all had this problem of interacting with you when you were a baby, kid, teenager, and adult. To handle you 'effectively' i.e. to their satisfaction, every one of them who interacted with you tried to mold you. Whatever you are today is largely the result of all those interactions as well as the learnings you did on your own. The way you think, feel, react, and express is the result of these learnings.

Let us say, you are a vegetarian, and while eating your food you suddenly realize that it has meat in it. Your reaction could vary from a gentle refusal to eat to that of vomiting. And the uneasy feeling might stay for a few minutes to days. It all depends on how you got trained. If you react to this situation without much thinking, then it is called "Conditioning". Most of your behavior is the result of this "Conditioning".

Let us take another example. If you are like many of us, you might associate yourself with a particular religion. And it is highly likely that you are very proud of YOUR religion even if you don't follow its strict rules or rituals. And there is also a possibility that you consider your religion to be superior to all other religions. Just bear with me for a minute. Take a deep breath and imagine a situation where you were brought up by parents of a religion that you particularly don't like. Imagine...

Will you be having the same negative feelings about that religion? Absolutely not!

This is the result of conditioning. Conditioning is both good and bad. It helps us by providing schemas to handle day-to-day situations easily. It takes away the burden of thinking and analyzing a situation every moment, and it provides immediate reaction. At the same time, it is bad if the conditioned reaction causes you harm or makes you unhappy. The nature of the conditioned response is such that you won't know it coming, it is automatic. This automatic response, this conditioned behavior that can harm you is the root cause of your unhappiness.

The way you dress up, the choice of food you eat, the way you take care of yourself, and the ideas of good or bad that you have; all are due to this conditioning. Dressing, for example, varies so much from one culture to the other. And you may find the dress sense of many cultures weird.

This phenomenon of conditioning was first discovered by the Russian Physiologist, *Ivan Pavlov,* during the 1890s. He has demonstrated this phenomenon through a famous experiment with a dog. This form of conditioning is known as Classical Conditioning. There are other forms of conditioning too by which all living organisms learn.

The challenge for us humans is to be able to overcome this conditioning and make a rational choice. As you might have realized by now most of our thinking, actions, and behavior are the result of our learning. To gain control over our thinking, and actions - in short over our mind - we have to unlearn a lot by deconditioning ourselves. Fortunately, I found a simple mechanism to de-condition. You need to follow that procedure to specifically work on each of those behaviors that you want to gain control over. After you learn the technique of deconditioning, you may start with the emotions that cause unhappiness to you.

## The Interactions

Let us now dissect what happens in an interaction with another person. When I said interaction, it could be a real interaction or imaginary i.e. thinking about interacting with a person in mind. After all, whatever happens is inside your mind. And the stimuli for your action can be external or internal.

The greatest challenge in interacting with another person is to make the other person do what we like or what we consider right. The other people in this situation can be your partner, your parents, your children, your siblings, friends, colleagues, etc. If the other person's actions are to our liking, we feel good. But you should also expect that the other people will have the same goal too, i.e., getting what they want. If your goals are not in sync, conflict arises and leads to unhappiness.

The first step towards gaining control is to break down your interactions into a unit that can be observable. Sounds technical? Yes, technical it is! The science of "Transactional Analysis (TA)" provides insight into the way we interact. According to this theory, every interaction can be broken down into a unit called "Transaction". In technical terms, a "Transaction" is a combination of "Stimulus" plus "Response".

In a mathematical representation:

**Transaction = Stimulus + Response**

An example of a Transaction:

A) How are you? (Stimulus)

B) I am fine, Thanks! (Response)

**Note:** A series of these transactions becomes an interaction.

The Stimulus could arise from the external environment, or from the inside. The way you respond to this Stimulus is Response. Whatever you have been doing in this life can be considered as a collection of all these "Responses". In a typical scenario, your responses are almost automatic. You know why. Whatever change or control you can bring in your life is by controlling these responses. For that to happen you should be aware of the way you Respond. To be aware, you need to ***pause*** the automatic response. This itself is a major challenge. The way to gain that control is through deconditioning.

Let us take a few examples with negative responses:

1. **Stimulus:** Your partner/kid is not obeying your command.

   **Your Response:** It could be anger, hopelessness, or frustration.

2. **Stimulus**: You come across an acquaintance who in the past hurt you by calling you names such as "idiot" or "dumb".

   **Your Response**: Again, it could be anger or rage.

3. **Stimulus:** Waiting for an important result of an exam you took, or for a diagnostic report of your health.

   **Your Response:** It could be anxiety, nervousness, or fear.

4. **Stimulus:** You must attend an important meeting or appear for an exam.

   **Your Response:** Again, it could be anxiety, nervousness, or fear.

5. **Stimulus:** At the dining table, one of your family members spills water on your dress

   **Your Response:** It could be anger or rage.

In each of the above situations, the responses noted above generate negative feelings in you (In case, you experience positive feelings as your response, thanks for reading my book even though you don't need to.) These negative feelings cause you unhappiness. In the case of water spilling on you, you are physically affected, and these negative feelings get added to the misery. ***Pause*** for a few seconds. Observe your feelings and observe their effect on your body.

- Your heart starts beating faster,
- Your muscles get tensed,

- You might shiver/tremble a little,
- You may experience sweating,
- You might feel blood gushing into your face,
- Your thinking might get clouded etc.

All these changes are the result of the above responses. I know in all of the above 5 situations, you are the affected party. But the question is:

Is your response helping you?

In fact, it is adding to your discomfort. It is taking away your happy moments. If you can recollect any previous instances like the above, you might have carried those negative feelings, unpleasantness, and discomfort for much longer than you anticipated. In some cases, a simple Stimulus of the above type might have led to a series of complicated negative interactions as well as outcomes.

In the cases of #1, #2, and #5, you might say "I want to teach a lesson to the other person". Yes, go ahead and teach a lesson. If you feel the need to be aggressive or angry to control others, do it! But without its adverse reactions on your body. You can always ACT aggressively/angrily without the accompanying heartbeat increase, adrenaline flowing, etc. Be ***selfishk***. Gain control of your bodily reactions, and exercise control over others whenever required.

Let us spend a few more minutes on the 5 cases above to look at the "Response". Because the "Response" is the ONLY thing you need to exercise your control over for life-long happiness. This moment of "Response" is the "Present". This is the moment you have to live. Everything before this and after this is NOT in your control.

Let us review all the above cases, briefly:

**In the case of #1,** you can take care of whatever you have asked your partner/kid to do. You can also think about how to make them act as per your wishes. You can also think of conditioning them.

**In the case of #2,** you can ignore the person and move on. In some cases, that itself becomes a powerful response. Or you can forgive the past behavior and respond positively. By this, you won't allow this present moment to be affected negatively by the past. You have already experienced hurt in the past, and any negative reaction now will add more unhappy moments to your life. Do you want to do that? Choose rationally.

**In the case of #3,** you will realize whatever the experience that you are going through is NOT going to change the outcome. And whatever the outcome is, the current suffering is adding more unhappiness moments.

**In the case of #4,** it is justified to be nervous, anxious, and fearful. Having these feelings at a moderate level might help you become more alert and more focused. But the excessive dose of these feelings will cloud your thinking and will work against your goals. What is moderate? And what is excessive? you need to identify. But it is good to prepare for the Future. How do we prepare? We will be discussing that in the next chapter.

**In the case of #5,** you need to clean yourself or you can make the other person do it for you. You can also decide how you want him/her to behave next time. If you think it is done on purpose, you can teach him a lesson, but without experiencing the accompanying negative bodily reactions.

I hope you got an understanding of Transaction, Stimulus, and Response, and the need for control over the Response. You will agree with me that...

> ***... the external stimuli are not the reason for your bodily reactions or feelings; it is your Response to the Stimuli.***

Your mind interprets the Stimuli in a certain way and sets the reactions. To control your Response, you need to be aware of what is going on inside of you. You should be able to observe your body's reactions. You should be able to notice your thoughts. For that to happen, you should learn to ***"Pause"*** between Stimulus and Response.

## Two Techniques that Help You to Pause

- **Slow Deep Breathing**
  ... for immediate short-term control
- **Relaxation**
  ... for long-term control

Both these are very powerful techniques to reverse the effects of stress such as tension and anxiety. You already know how your feelings result in bodily changes. Your thoughts and your feelings have an immediate effect on your body. The emotions that lead to stress have serious negative consequences on your physical body. Numerous studies and experiments prove that stress leads to various physical ailments. These ailments are referred to as ***Psychosomatic disorders.*** Just by gaining control over your emotions, you can bring in considerable improvement in your general well-being. Time and again it has been proved that positive thoughts/feelings help your body stay in good condition. This is how the Zillion types of prayers and rituals help people feel better. Whatever the method or ritual you follow, the underlying positive emotion leads to a better feeling. Some of the tasks suggested by Positive Psychology fit into this explanation e.g. Doing 3 good things, showing gratitude, putting beach rocks one over the other, etc.

One of the most illustrative effects of mind over body is our "fight-or-flight" response. Whenever you face a threatening situation, this response gets triggered. This is the result of the "Sympathetic Nervous System (SNS)". It prepares you by boosting your heart rate and respiratory rate, and by sending extra blood to muscles. This makes you respond immediately. To "**Pause**" your response, you need to undo the effects of SNS. Luckily, our human body has a counter mechanism called the "Parasympathetic Nervous System (PNS)". You can trigger this system ***voluntarily*** through slow breathing and relaxation.

***Breathing and Relaxation are the only 2 techniques that allow you to control your mind.***

All the Meditation and mind-soothing practices are built using these 2 primary techniques.

## Slow Deep Breathing

You can use this technique to calm your nerves and regain your composure. To learn to **"Pause"** before you respond, take a deep breath slowly. This act of taking slow deep breaths triggers the PNS and helps in bringing down your heart rate and controlling blood flow. This, in turn, results in a calmer mind. And allows you to "***Choose***" your reaction. You must make an effort to learn it.

Are you ready?

Sit straight. Take a slow deep breath. Close your mouth, breathe in & breathe out through both nostrils.

1. First fill the bottom part of your lungs. For this you should do Diaphragm breathing i.e. when you inhale, your belly should protrude. Try it.
2. While holding that, fill the middle part of the lungs, by pushing your chest out.
3. Finally, fill the upper part of the lungs by raising your shoulders upwards.
4. Hold your breath for a few seconds (Count to 4; 1, 2, 3, 4).
5. Now, exhale in the same order - pull in your belly, collapse your chest, and lower your shoulders, slowly (Again count for 4; 1, 2, 3, 4).

Repeat this 3 times and feel the calming effect. Apart from calming your mind, it has many positive effects on your body.

Practice this conscious slow breathing. Take slow deep breaths throughout the day, whenever possible. You can do it in private, and you can do it in public too (it is hardly noticeable). In meditation practices, there are lots of variations on how long you hold the breath, how fast you breathe, etc.

Practice taking deep slow breaths, so that you can immediately relax when a need arises. Whenever you think your body is showing signs of rage, blood gushing, nervousness, or your mind is getting slammed with many thoughts or repetitive thoughts, take slow deep breaths - at least 3 times. This will help you calm down a little, hopefully, that **"Pause"** is enough for you to make the right choice that stops unhappy moments and may help you convert it to happy moments.

Especially when you are sad and feeling low, slow deep breaths will make you feel better. After that, a technique I use in those situations is to act as if I were in a good mood such as singing a song and dancing a jig. Eventually, these physical actions influence my mood and my mood changes for the better. Mind you, in the case of chronic sadness you must see a Counselor.

## Relaxation

As we discussed earlier, your mind can cause physical problems for you. The stress you experience can result in Psychosomatic disorders such as Ulcers, Skin rashes, high blood pressure, back pain, irritable bowel; and in aggravating existing conditions such as heart disease, cancer, etc.

As you know when you are under stress, your mind gets clouded, and the decisions or actions you take may not be in your best interest. So, in those situations, it becomes a tough challenge to choose the options that can help you live happily. For you to live happily, it is of utmost importance that you learn to be stress-free. The technique of relaxation helps you in that effort. The technique is simple and easy to practice, and it takes just about 15 minutes. This is the same technique used by all the meditative and spiritual processes. Many Gurus and Spiritual leaders have included this in their practice by tweaking it here and there; and built it over by including imagery and breathing techniques.

The basic technique of relaxation is as follows:

1. Your goal is to relax all your body muscles and keep your mind calm.
2. You should learn to be aware of the tightening of your muscles and the relaxed state of your muscles. [As an exercise, right now just focus on your facial muscles. Can you relax them? Did you notice the tense state before you relaxed them? Try that with your shoulder muscles and feel the muscles loosening up.]
3. Lie down on your back on a comfortable mat or bed.
4. Now start focusing on one set of muscles at a time. You should tighten that set of muscles and relax them. Focus your mind on how those muscles feel. You have to train your mind to learn to notice the state of tension vs relaxation in those muscles. ***Being aware of how relaxed muscles feel is the key.*** The more you train, the easier it will be for you to relax those muscles quickly at will.
5. Start from toe to head. Keep focusing on a set of muscles - tighten, count to four, release, and relax to the extent possible. Now keep going up from toe to head. Technically it is called PMR (Progressive Muscle Relaxation), colloquially body scan relaxation.
6. Now repeat it 3 times. As you continue to practice, you will be able to relax muscles very quickly, and easily.

7. Now tell yourself to Relax. While relaxing your muscles, tell yourself "Relax! Relax! Relax!". Now focus on relaxing the entire body. Scan your body and identify the muscles that are tight and relax them. Continue to tell yourself "Relax! Relax! Relax!".
8. Now that you have gained some control over noticing your body muscles, switch your focus to your breathing. While you are aware of your body muscles condition, take slow deep breaths. If you learned diaphragm breathing, your belly would move rhythmically. Watch your breath and observe your belly and chest movements. While doing all this, keep saying "Relax! Relax! Relax!". With each inhalation, tell yourself you are relaxing deeper and deeper. With each exhalation, tell yourself all your tensions are going away.
9. To relax further, add imagery to this practice. Many spiritual Gurus and Hypnotists take the help of imagery to put you into a deeper relaxation state. You can use the same technique to help yourself relax deeper. So, imagine yourself in a place that gives you happiness. While in a relaxed state, imagine yourself enjoying that place.
10. To come out of this relaxation process, slowly tighten your muscles from toe to head and stretch as if you were getting out of sleep.

Practice this relaxation as detailed above. Your mind gets expert at relaxing your muscles in the same way it got trained for cycling or swimming. It becomes a skill that you can use in whatever situation you are in. This improves your physical health, your capacity to "**Pause**", your ability to calm your mind, your ability to focus/concentrate, and your ability to "**Choose**" actions that benefit you. Thus, you gain control over your conditioned responses.

In my view, the discovery of the phenomenon of "Conditioning" by Ivan Pavlov is the greatest contribution to the science of Psychology. What you are today can be explained largely by understanding how you got conditioned. Similarly, you can know others well if you make an effort to understand their conditioning. It will help you deal with them effectively. Try paying attention to others' conditioning. Understanding their conditioning helps you to empathize with them. Empathizing improves your interactions. And if you learned about the process of conditioning, you could utilize some of the techniques to deal with others for your ***selfishk*** benefit.

> With the power of "**Pause**" and "**Choose**", you can now decide what you want to do at that moment as well as plan for your future.

As discussed above, every "Transaction" is a part of an interaction. And the interactions will lead to a relationship. Similarly, every step you take at this moment is a step towards your goals. So, let us now look at how you can plan to achieve your goals, in short, plan for your future.

---***---

# Chapter #7

# Preparing Yourself for the Future

The power of "**Pause & Choose**" entrusts you with greater responsibility. Whatever the action you take, you choose that action, so you have no one else to blame. It is you who must own up to the consequences. Mistakes may happen; it is possible that things won't work the way you planned. The best you can do is to learn from those mistakes and going forward "**Choose**" another well-evaluated response. Keep this learning process alive. You will become a better decision-maker. And it makes your life interesting too.

EVERY moment in our life is a decision-making moment. We are, continually, forced to think and prioritize what to do. It is always a compromise, and we have to choose one from among many options/paths available to us. It is the reality that we CANNOT do everything we want to do, and we should feel okay with it. I agree all of us have many things to achieve in life. But we have to realize that it is futile to attempt to achieve everything. We are constrained by the practical limitations of time and energy. The best thing we can do is to **PRIORITIZE** what we want to achieve to maximize our life goals. We should live in such a way that at any point in time, we achieve the maximum.

Does it sound overwhelming?

As you learn and condition yourself in a way that benefits you, you will respond with ease. Most of your actions become automatic, you will have to "**Pause & Choose**" in lesser and lesser situations. Overall, your happiness moments increase. And you may even add more happy moments to your near and dear.

To achieve your goals, you need to have a well-laid-out strategy. Mathematics and problem-solving techniques help us with this.

**There are 2 things that you need to do:**

1. **Plan all your steps to achieve your goal.**
2. **Excel in executing the current step.**

## 1. Plan All Your Steps to Achieve Your Goal:

Do you love Mathematics? Many people don't. But Mathematics shows the way to solve real-life problems too. The strategy we use to solve a mathematical problem can be applied to real-life problems too. Let me explain this process with an example:

**Problem:** Find the cost of tiles required to cover a flooring of size 20 ft. by 20 ft. Each tile has a size of 2 ft. by 2 ft. The cost per tile is $1.

**Plan:** Based on the information provided (one of the strategies):

- We have to first find out how many tiles are required to cover the flooring. Then we can arrive at the total cost.
- To find the number of tiles, we have to find the area of the flooring. Then divide that area by the area of a tile.

**Solution step-by-step:**

1. Total area of the flooring
   = 20 ft. X 20 ft. = 400 sq. ft.
2. Area of one tile = 2 ft. X 2 ft. = 4 sq. ft.
3. Number of tiles required
   = 400 sq. ft. / 4 sq. ft. = 100
4. Total cost of tiles = 100 X $1 = $100
5. The answer is $100

To solve this problem, we have first formulated a strategy. The plan contains the steps required to arrive at a solution. It is assumed that you know the formula for the area of a Square, which is "side X side". Then we solved the problem step-by-step and arrived at the solution in step #4.

The first thing here is laying out the strategy. To do that you should have enough knowledge of the problem domain. For example, in this case, knowing the area of the Square is important. If you are not conversant with this type of problem, the best recourse for you is to reach out to knowledgeable people. It could be your friends, family members, or experts in that area.

It is the same with life's problems. Let us say you have a relationship problem, a problem appearing for an exam, a financial problem, or a major health issue. Consider it as the mathematics problem discussed above and theorize how that can be solved. If you cannot arrive at a plan or strategy to solve it, reach out to experts.

- Deliberate about various possible solutions,
- Choose the one that you consider works best,
- And identify the steps in that solution.

You should have confidence that your plan works. During execution, if you get additional information, validate your steps and make mid-course corrections. Otherwise, follow the steps wholeheartedly. Let us apply this to the real-life problems mentioned above and look at them briefly.

- **Relationship problem:** Find out why you have this problem. Let us assume the other person is at fault. See how you can let the other person know about it. Will shouting at the person work? Will reason out, work? Or will a trusted friend explain it, works?

  If you are at fault - will apologizing work? Will buying a gift work? Or will undoing whatever the damage, work? Decide and prepare a plan.

- **Appearing for an exam:** Find out what all that you need to prepare. Find out how much time you have for preparation. See if you need guidance or help from others. See if the available time is sufficient to cover all the material that you need to study. Find out what other options you have for getting more time. Do you think postponing taking the exam by a few days works? Think and chalk out a detailed plan about how to spend your time every day.

- **A financial problem**: Assess the nature of the problem. How much money and how fast do you need? Find out who can help you with money, and how much they can contribute. Find out if you need to sell any assets you have. Find out what are the things you have to forgo. Decide on the best course available and lay out the steps to implement the same.

- **A major health problem:** How serious is the health problem? What options are available for a cure? How much money does it cost? What are the ways to arrange the money? Can you delay the treatment? Or is there a cure for it? Consult specialists and experts. Gain knowledge. Discuss with the people concerned and decide on the course of action that you consider the best. Figure out what you have to do immediately.

Finding a strategy/plan becomes difficult and complicated, when you do not know if the decision you are taking is the best, or if you have to forgo one thing that you love for another you love equally.

## 2. Excel in Executing the Current Step:

After you have a plan, the next important thing is to act on the immediate step. In our Mathematics example, the key thing that you have to note is that when you were at Step #1, you did not know what the result would be at Step #4.

***Your focus was always on the step you were working on.***

You were confident that if you followed your strategy you would arrive at the result.

After you have completed Step #1, you have focused on Step #2. Again, at this stage also, you were not aware of the final result. And you were very aware that if you complete each step correctly, you will arrive at the correct result. At Step #2, for all practical purposes, you did not worry about the result of the previous step, and you were not anxious about the future steps. You just wanted to get Step #2 done correctly.

You should have this same attitude while solving your real-life problems.

***Once you have made a well-thought-out decision and prepared a plan, just focus on the immediate step.***

Not to look back, or not to look too far into the future. In a way, do not worry about the past, and do not get anxious about the future. Just do what you think would take you to the goal. Now all your energies should be focused on getting the current step executed effectively.

I am sure you already know this process of breaking down the problem into steps and handling it one at a time. Despite knowing that, many of us get stressed-out/burned out in our daily lives. The reason - we have to handle/juggle many problems at a time. While we are trying to focus on one problem, the other problems too force themselves into our minds and **vie for attention.** This disturbs our minds, and we tend to go crazy. There is a simple technique to overcome this problem. It is known as **Time-boxing.**

**Handling multiple tasks effectively**

Most of our life situations DO NOT require immediate action. You can plan and handle them one after the other. But many times, at work as well as at home, we might be pushed to act on a task immediately. We get into the urgency mode due to the pressure we experience.

One of the main reasons for the stress that we experience while performing a task is **the awareness of other things that we have to do.** So, we tend to attend to more than one task at the same time. Let us say,

- you have to go for a health check-up.
- You have to go to a party.
- You have to buy a few things.
- You want to know the result of an important decision [such as an election result, the result of your application for a job or admission into a college].
- You have to complete a work-related task.
- Etc.

In a normal situation, while we are handling a work-related task, the awareness of all the other tasks pushes us to rush through the current task. We keep reminding ourselves of all other things that we are supposed to take care of. So, while taking care of the work-related task, we might want to take unscheduled breaks to squeeze in the sub-tasks of other activities, such as:

- Call the Doctor's office.
- Talk to the guys who are hosting the party.
- Go out of the office and buy a couple of things.
- Check the site that provides the outcome of the result you are waiting for.

By juggling all these activities at the same time, we get a sense of accomplishing a lot in a short time. So, we get into the habit of multi-tasking to FEEL that we are being more productive. This juggling of many things at a time leads to stress, not only due to the energy required to handle them but also for the fear of dropping one of them unintentionally.

The alternative way to accomplish all your tasks without stress is Time-boxing**. It means you need to ALLOCATE a certain amount of time for each of those tasks**. And you will take up a particular task only during that allocated time. In the above example, you can decide that you will take a break from the work-related task from 2 pm to 3 pm. You will decide that only during that time you will call the doctor's office and talk to the guy hosting the party. If you have some more time left, you will go and buy a few things from your list. And about checking the status of the result, you might NOT check unless you need to act on the result immediately. With this approach, you will be focusing on one task at a time. As you decide to take a break between 2 pm and 3 pm, you will be fully focusing on the work-related task. Due to that, you would be more productive and you would be doing your best. Most importantly you feel less stressed out as you know you won't be dropping any task as you have set aside time for everything.

**Avoid multitasking.**
**Embrace Time-boxing!**

Let us look at a few examples of how Time-boxing can benefit you.

**Ex. 1:** You are planning for a trip abroad. Let us say, you need to take the Visa, book a hotel, book tickets, pack your stuff, and make arrangements to take care of your home in your absence. Decide on the sequence of activities and their dependencies. If getting a Visa is essential to make all other arrangements, you should schedule all other tasks for a later date and should think about them **during their allotted time slots ONLY**.

**Ex. 2:** You want to apply for a college admission or a job. Let us say, you have to identify the colleges/jobs, short-list them, find out the requirements for each of them, prepare your resume accordingly, pay the fees, submit the application, and wait for the outcome. Schedule your work as per the timelines of institutions, and **do not think about the tasks till you get into that time box**. Check the status of your application **during the time specified by the institutions.** It is futile and unnecessary to keep checking every day. Just pay attention to your emails.

**Ex. 3:** A simple one. Check your work-related emails only **during the timebox that you have allocated for it**. Do not get tempted to read every email as soon as you receive it.

**Enjoy doing the task on hand:**

As we discussed a couple of times earlier in the book, all your living is in the present i.e., in this very moment. Whatever you do at this very moment defines your life. The past and the future can only guide you to what you need to do NOW. So, your focus should be only on the task you have at hand. The techniques we discussed for gaining control over your mind, namely - slow breathing and relaxation - come in handy. Whatever the task that you need to do, focus on excelling in that. We learned in the earlier chapter **"Cross the 7 steps"** that no task is inferior. If you have to do it, you have to do it to the best of your ability. That is the way to enjoy the task at hand.

***Do everything possible at your command to excel. Then every task becomes enjoyable.***

You might have heard about Mindfulness, flow, etc. It has been observed that people who get immersed in a task experience extreme joy and happiness. They might become completely oblivious of the surroundings e.g., a musician playing an instrument, an artist painting a picture, a person solving a puzzle, a teenager playing a video game, a kid watching a cartoon show, or a devotee praying to God. Even when you call out their names, they may not respond. It is as if they were in a trance. **This state of focus and concentration is called "flow". The ability to be in that frame of mind is known as "Mindfulness".** For all of them, time stands still. They may not realize how much time has passed. They associate these moments with extreme joy and happiness.

One of the ways to enjoy life is to be able to get into that state with everyday tasks too. You should learn to immerse yourself in the activity at hand and pay full attention to the task at hand. Whether it is taking a bath, eating your food, cleaning the toilets, doing your work at your office, studying a book, playing a game, or learning something new; whatever it may be all your senses should be focused on that.

To reach that level of control over your mind, you need to de-condition yourself of old habits and learn new ways of doing things. The next chapter is about that.

**Why excelling at a task is so satisfying?**

Reason - it becomes **"Play".**

By nature, we long for improvement. In a play, you can observe your performance, and you will strive to improve it. The key factor in playing is the small immediate goals that you have. So, at every short interval, you can measure your performance and can try to excel next time. You get many chances to do that without losing anything permanently.

If you take your work as play and focus on excelling, you will enjoy that activity. As in play, you can see the improvement in yourself, and feel good about the progress. To make work interesting, convert it into a play. For example, if you want kids to clean up their room, you can convert that activity into play. You can say, for example, "Let us see how many things each one of you can set right. The time starts now!".

---***---

# Chapter #8
# Lay the Foundation

In this Chapter, you are going to learn **the simple technique** for deconditioning. This is the foundation for building your happiness world.

Let us look at a very common emotion "anger". We all know why anger is bad, and why forgiving is good. When you don't get angry, and forgive a person, it might appear to outsiders that you are behaving saintly. But in reality, you are just being ***selfishk.*** Anger pushes your body and mind into an agitated state, leading to damage to your system. On the other hand, forgiving relieves you of all those problems, and restores your system to some extent. For many of us, the emotion of anger is an automatic response. The challenge is, gaining control over it. Similar to this emotion of anger, most of our responses are automatic. And we know that this is due to the conditioning. And many negative emotions such as remorse, worry, anxiety, sorrow, pain, hopelessness, fear, etc., will come in the way of our happiness. This chapter is about gaining control over those emotions and replacing them with less damaging or neutral responses. This skill needs to be mastered. And there is one technique that will help you in that effort of deconditioning.

As I have mentioned in the Prologue, I have applied this technique to gain control over my emotions and reached the stage of being happy almost all the time. It is a simple technique but needs to be applied consciously for each of those negative behaviors that you want to overcome. How fast and how effectively you gain control depends entirely on you. The more creative you become, and the more determined you are, the better for you. As stated earlier, it would take a good amount of time to reach a stage that you consider being at peace with yourself, and in full control of your emotions.

Realize that since childhood you have been conditioned to react in a particular way by your parents, teachers, and by society. So, you need to understand YOUR CONDITIONING i.e., YOUR impulsive reactions to events. To overcome this conditioning, as we discussed in an earlier chapter, you need to practice "**Pause & Choose**" instead of immediate reaction.

***In every situation,***

- **PAUSE and THINK about all the actions you can take.**
- **CHOOSE the one that retains or gives you happiness.**

Even though this process has only TWO steps, you need lots and lots of practice.

Let us take an example to understand what goes on in a situation where you get victimized and unhappy. Let us say your partner or significant other calls you often dumb & idiot. Every time the person says you are dumb & idiot; you might get offended and might get mad at that person. One of the actions you can take is "Ignoring the person completely". If you allow yourself to get angry and feel miserable then you have given the power to your partner to take away your happiness. Let us say that despite you showing your anger or pleading, your partner does not change his/her behavior. Then, you become a victim.

**So, when you are unable to control the other person's behavior, and unable to control your negative reactions, you become the victim**. Your partner can effectively utilize this phenomenon to hurt you again and again. So, in a way, you get into a trap. For all practical reasons, your partner intends to hurt you, and you are obliging willingly. What is happening here? You have given control over your happiness to your partner.

In our daily lives, we will come across many people who want to control us and our happiness by design or by their conditioning. As you have decided to be happy in every situation, you should retain control over your emotions. You do not want anyone to take away your happiness. If required, you can decide to teach a lesson to your victimizer while keeping your happiness intact. But to react in this way, you should come out of your conditioning. The one technique of deconditioning that I have been referring to is:

**"EXPERIMENT"** -
The Mantra for Emotional Control!

This is the technique that helps you decondition and gain control over your emotions. This technique helps you get desensitized to negativity and thus puts you in charge of your actions by allowing you to choose your response.

To understand this concept, let us look at how desensitization works in the case of phobia treatment. Let us say Mr. X has a phobia of snakes i.e., Ophiophobia. Whenever the thought of a snake comes to his mind, his body shows the symptoms of fear, and he feels very frightened. A phobia as you know is an irrational/abnormal fear. How he developed this fear is not of importance to us, but we know he got CONDITIONED to respond in this way. The desensitization technique can help him overcome this conditioning.

The desensitization process focuses on getting Mr. X to overcome his fear in a series of steps from the least disturbing to the most disturbing. The key factor in this whole process is making Mr. X **"learn to relax"** while he is exposed to the disturbing stimulus. The process starts with the low-risk exposure.

In a typical case, the process can contain the following steps:

1. A drawing of a snake is shown to Mr. X. If he exhibits symptoms of fear or anxiety, he is asked to relax by slow deep breathing and by consciously relaxing his body. [Refer to the previous chapter about these 2 techniques]. This process is repeated till he overcomes the anxiety response to the snake's drawing.
2. A photo of the snake is shown to Mr. X. Again, the same exposure and relaxation process is repeated till he overcomes the negative response. This process is repeated at every other step that follows this step.
3. Mr. X is asked to touch the photo.
4. ... is shown a video of the snake.
5. ... is asked to touch the video.
6. ... is shown a live snake enclosed in a glass chamber.
7. ... is asked to touch the glass chamber.
8. ... is shown a snake made of cloth.
9. ... is asked to touch and then hold the snake made of cloth.
10. ...is shown a snake made of rubber that resembles a real-life snake.
11. ... is asked to touch and then hold the realistic rubber snake.
12. ... is shown a real snake.
13. Finally, Mr. X is asked to touch the real snake and then hold it. This act confirms his overcoming of fear/phobia of snakes.

As you can see, he has to go through many steps in a gradual manner of exposure to higher-risk stimuli. This is called ***"Systematic desensitization"***. How fast he overcomes depends entirely on his ability to practice relaxation. All through this process he has to undo the earlier conditioning and replace it with relaxed state feelings.

I call each of these steps an "***Experiment***". You do an Experiment to help you decondition yourself of a particular response. You may repeat the Experiment or modify it as necessary. Let us look at the concept of Experiment closely.

**EXPERIMENT**

1. *It is a voluntary setup.*
2. *You decide what should be the stimulus.*
3. *You decide the time and place for trying it out.*
4. *You decide when to stop.*
5. *Your goal of the experiment is to stay calm and relaxed when exposed to the stimulus. You will apply slow breathing and relaxation techniques.*
6. *Most importantly, a failure, i.e., not getting the desired response, is also a success.*
7. *You will try to stay calm in the case of not getting the desired response too.*

Review step #3 above of Mr. X. All that we explained about the Experiment applies. Even though Mr. X's goal is to touch the photo of a snake without having any negative symptoms, his attempt to touch the photo itself is a success. His mental preparation to do that Experiment itself is a step towards his final goal. Every time he repeats this Experiment, he gets a chance to review and modify his thinking and his relaxing techniques. However small the improvement is, it becomes a layer in the foundation for the final goal. The stronger the negative reaction, the deeper the foundation will be i.e., it requires many layers of small improvements. It is very important to notice the minute improvements and feel good about them. This will in turn become a strong motivation to continue that process.

Hope you understand what an Experiment is! For every behavior that you want to work on, you should design Experiments. The challenge here is to become very creative and design appropriate Experiments. Let us apply this technique to the 5 situations we discussed in a previous chapter.

1. **Stimulus:** Your partner/kid not obeying your command.

   **Your Response:** It could be anger, hopelessness, or frustration.

   **Experiments:**
   a. **Lowest risk:** When no one is around, even though you don't need it, ask your partner/kid to do a task. If you don't get a proper response, stay calm by doing slow-breathing. Move on to the next step only when you can stay relaxed. Repeat the same with the next steps.
   b. **Low risk:** Do the same when a few other close family members are there. Stay calm if you do not get a proper response.
   c. **Medium risk:** Repeat the same when you are with family and friends.
   d. **High risk:** Do the same at a party.

   [**Note:** *Once you master staying calm, you can try different ways to get your work done* e.g., *Change your tone, raise your voice.*]

2. **Stimulus:** You come across an acquaintance who in the past hurt you by calling you names such as "idiot" or "dumb".

   **Your Response:** It could be anger or rage.

   **Experiments:**

   a. **Lowest risk:** Think of the person and imagine meeting him. Move on to the next step only when you can stay relaxed. Do slow breathing for relaxation. Repeat the same with the next steps.
   b. **Low risk:** When alone, look at that person's photo and say aloud what you want to say.
   c. **Medium risk:** Tell your close friend/partner how you will react when you meet this person.
   d. **High risk:** Plan a situation in such a way that you meet this person. In that meeting, the other person might again insult you. But, if you stay relaxed and calm, you win.

   [**Note:** Remember, you may not always get the expected result from others. You may not have control over their behavior. The key thing here is that you are gaining control over your own emotions and behavior. As you practice this control more, you may learn techniques to control others' behavior too.]

3. **Stimulus:** Waiting for an important result of an exam you took, or for a diagnostic report of your health

**Your Response:** It could be anxiety, nervousness, or fear.

**Experiments:**

a. **Low risk:** Take an exam, say a free online one, that you know you will ace. For a diagnostic report, take a test to know your blood group. And don't look at the result for a few days. [And you know what all you need to do in an Experiment. So, I will skip repeating them].
b. **Medium risk:** Take an exam, say a free online one, that you do not need, but you are sure you won't get full marks. For a diagnostic report, take a simple blood test. And don't look at the result for a few days. If you want, you can inform significant others about these tests.
c. **High risk:** Take an exam that is of importance to you. For a diagnostic report, go for your regular check-up. And wait for a few days before you look at the results.

4. **Stimulus:** You must attend an important meeting or appear for an exam.

   **Your Response:** Again, it could be anxiety, nervousness, or fear.

   **Experiments:**

   a. **Low risk:** Set up a meeting with your subordinates to share your knowledge on a specific topic you are comfortable with.

      Sign up for an exam that is not very important to you. And inform your close friends and family members about it.

b. **Medium risk:** Set up a meeting with your subordinates to share your knowledge on a topic that is important for the team.

   Sign up for an exam which is very important to you.

c. **High risk:** Set up a meeting with your peers to share your knowledge on a topic that is important for all of them.

   Sign up for an exam which is very important to you. And inform your close friends and family members about it.

5. **Stimulus:** At the dining table, one of your family members, spills water on your dress

   **Your Response:** It could be anger or rage.

   **Experiments:**

   a. **Lowest risk:** While at home, when no one is watching spill water on your dress. Stay with the dress on for a few minutes, say 10 minutes. Clean yourself.
   b. **Low risk:** While at home, when everyone is watching, enact a scene where you spill water on your dress. Clean it and stay calm.
   c. **Medium risk:** At dinner time, ask one of your family members to spill water on your dress. Stay calm and clean it.
   d. **High risk:** At a party, intentionally spill some

water on your dress. Clean it up and stay calm throughout the party.

Do these cases give you an idea of what you need to do for deconditioning?

**To gain control over your emotions i.e., to improve your response to a particular stimulus:**

- *Decide on the conditioning that you want to overcome, or in other terms - the behavior that you want to change.*
- *Create an Experiment i.e., create a situation that triggers that behavior.*
- *Learn to stay calm and relaxed. Do slow-deep-breathing.*
- *Try replacing the old action/behavior with the one you want.*

Think of your unhappy moments. See if you could have done something different. Decide what control you want to gain, and devise Experiments for them.

**Enjoying Life:**

You can use this technique of gaining control over your emotions, to indulge in happiness tasks too, and to enjoy life. You can devise Experiments to start enjoying life more, little by little. Be ***selfishk***, try those things that give you happiness. Say, you want to go alone to a restaurant and enjoy a feast. You can start with having an ice cream or a light snack that you enjoy.

Do you like the spa?

Or just want to take a relaxing bath in the tub?

Whatever it is, think of an Experiment and try it out. Do not feel guilty about wasting time or money. It is your life, and you have every right to enjoy yourself as long as you are not hurting yourself or others.

I am listing down some negative and positive behaviors that you may want to change. Add to the list or delete it from the list as appropriate. Devise Experiments and gain success.

**Overcoming Negative Feelings:**

- Not getting angry
- Working on cleanliness obsession
- Not getting annoyed by the behavior of your loved ones – Being ***selfishk.***
- Getting your hands and body dirty by doing physical activity, such as gardening
- Cleaning Toilets
- Tearing a favorite photo
- Giving away a favorite item

- Going out wearing the worst dress
- Not doing a particular ritual
- Not reacting negatively to cuss words

**Indulging in Activities that Give You Positive Feelings (Just Being *Selfishk*):**

- Take a day off without any specific reason, and just to while away the time.
- Call up a friend or relative with whom you enjoy talking.
- Appreciate someone for their help.
- Have fun alone, chilling out in a restaurant alone or visiting a sightseeing place such as a museum alone.
- Buy something for yourself.
- Practice Digital Detox for a day.
- Say NO to a person of importance.
- Mindfully enjoy a routine task such as taking a bath or eating food.
- Play a game with kids just for fun, without focusing on winning.
- Do an activity that you love but stopped doing due to daily pressures, such as drawing, painting, playing a musical instrument, etc.

I hope the above two lists give you a sense of the effort involved in working on deconditioning! It is simple and easy to work on one behavior at a time. But to be happy all the time, we need to Decondition many things. It is time-consuming. Keep working on one behavior, one situation at a time. Make your list of top priority behaviors that you want to gain control over. Be very creative, design Experiments and try one after the other till you succeed.

**Deconditioning requires strong determination and creativity. So, *people prefer rituals* that can Condition them to live in the "*Maya*" - the illusion.**

It is your choice. Decide wisely. Get real medicine instead of a placebo.

All this while, we have discussed the situations that you create to perform an Experiment. With that experience, you can face your real-life situations confidently. The process of Experimentation trains you to prepare in advance for a situation. Over some time, it helps you to develop the mindset of "**Pause & Choose**" - the all-important skill for handling real-life situations.

***Pause & Choose***

***You should train yourself to THINK rather than react, in every situation.***

- *THINK whether you have any means of control.*
- *If you cannot control it, ACCEPT it and be prepared for the worst.*
- *If you can control, THINK about all the possible options and their consequences.*
- *THINK about the worst outcome for each option.*
- *Choose the option based on your preparedness for the worst.*

To overcome deeply rooted negative behaviors, you might have to dig deep into your mind to unearth the conditioning. Layer by layer you have to decondition to overcome the negative behavior. This technique of "Experiment" lays the strong foundation to build the "4 Pillars of Happiness" that we are going to discuss in the next chapter.

---***---

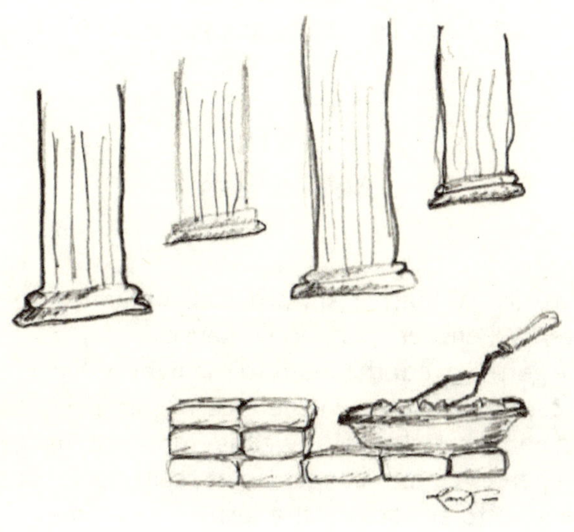

# Chapter #9
# Build the 4 Pillars

I hope you have started applying the Decondition technique to gain control over your emotions. It takes time to gain mastery over emotions. Try "**Experimenting**" with the least complicated situations, and experience success. It will bolster your confidence and will motivate you to go after bigger challenges.

For everlasting happiness, there are four aspects of life one needs to have control over. I call them "**4 Pillars of Happiness**". These *Four Pillars* are required to support your happiness world. To build these pillars you need to apply the technique learned in the chapter - “Lay the Foundation”. It means applying the Decondition technique effectively to overcome emotions related to each pillar. Let us look at each of them in detail.

## 1$^{st}$ Pillar
## Be Fearless

Fear is a survival mechanism provided by nature to protect ourselves. Whenever our body senses danger, the fear response gets evoked. This leads to the fight-or-flight response to take care of ourselves in the face of perceived danger. It results in both physiological as well as emotional changes. If the situation perceived as a danger is not really dangerous and/or not amenable to any action, the response becomes futile and results in unnecessary stress.

As we grew up, we have been conditioned intentionally or unintentionally, to be afraid of many things in life. A few people in society might have instilled fear in us to obey their orders, and/or we might have developed a fear of certain things in life. It is important to identify these fears and work on getting rid of them. Being fearless opens doors for greater joy and happiness.

The fears could be irrational (means imaginary) or rational (means real danger). To overcome irrational fears, sometimes called phobias, you should straight away apply the Decondition technique. If the irrational fears become unmanageable you must seek professional help. For rational fears, you should prepare an action plan to mitigate the risks and be prepared for the worst outcome. The main difference between irrational and rational fear lies in the possibility of the event happening. For example, someone being afraid of drowning while taking a shower can be classified as an irrational fear. On the other hand, a person being afraid of drowning in a river or in a swimming pool can be classified as rational fear.

Fear, if not managed, stops us from achieving our goals as well as enjoying our lives to the full extent. It becomes a major hurdle in being proactive and sometimes can force us to make decisions that are detrimental to us. Not just the defined goals, it can come in the way of day-to-day activities too. Because of the fears, we might end up spending more energy and more money than is reasonable. Let me explain with a couple of examples:

1. Let us say, you are standing in a queue at a coffee shop, and you are the 10th person in the line. Suddenly, you notice a person cutting the line and joining the queue in the middle. If you get angry, and if you do not ask him to join the queue at the end, it is an indication of fear. If you do not take any action, you will feel victimized and end up in 11th position.

2. Let us take another example. Say, you are visiting a new place - say a town in India. You are not sure about the exact location of a particular place that you want to visit. You can either ask a person for the directions, or you can spend time going around the place to figure it out on your own. For any reason, if you refrain from asking directions, that is again an indication of fear, and you end up spending more time and energy.

3. You come across a person doing a great service. You wanted to appreciate him/her but decided not to do it.

4. You see a person struggling with a particular task, on the road, in a mall, or in the office. You want to help but do not take the initiative.

5. You are at work, and you have a solution to a problem that your team is working on. You are in a meeting to discuss ways to address that problem, but you hesitate to share your solution.

6. You are at work, and you are struggling with a problem. You know that the guy next to you knows the solution, but you decide not to take his help.

Even these small acts of **refrain** fall under the category of fear. You may not have realized how many times in a day you refrain from doing or saying something that **<u>you want to</u>**. Think about it! Think about yesterday. Go through the entire day's activities in your mind and see how many times you STOPPED from doing or saying something even though you wanted to do or say. If you did STOP, then consider that some unknown FEAR has stopped you.

In the earlier days of my journey on this path of happiness, I realized that I was getting scared as many as 10 to 12 times a day. That FEAR was stopping me from taking action. Due to that, I could not get many things completed as well as could not go after the things that I wanted to. Realizing that I decided to become FEARLESS. Toward that goal, I applied the 'Mantra of Deconditioning' - EXPERIMENT. As I started overcoming one fear after the other my life had become more enjoyable. As you might agree, gaining control over emotions, particularly overcoming all fears, cannot happen overnight. I spent many years identifying my fears, planning Experiments, and trying them out again and again till I got full control.

Let us briefly revisit the above four cases and see how Experimenting plays in those situations. In all those cases, if you take action, you will realize that you WILL NOT lose anything (except some money in a few cases). The reasoning is as follows. Let me illustrate it with the 1st case of you standing in a queue. Consider this as an Experiment. As you might remember, failing to get the desired outcome is also a success in the Experiment. Just to reiterate, you should stay calm even in the face of failure.

1. First, you should decide what you are going to say to the person who is cutting the line.
2. Think about all possible consequences.
3. Find out what is the WORST possible outcome.
4. See if you can handle the WORST consequence.
5. If yes, go ahead with your action.
6. If no (say, you think he might physically assault you), accept the fact of being 11th in the queue and stay calm.

> **"In many cases,**
> **the WORST outcome puts you in the**
> **<u>same status as you were</u>**
> **before you initiated the action"**

In this case, when the person joined the queue in the middle, your position changed to 11th position. Let us say you initiated the action, but the person did not heed your request. So, you will remain in the 11th position itself. There is no change in status. If you try doing this, say on 3 or 4 different occasions, there is a possibility of you succeeding once or twice. That is overall positive.

Think about all those day-to-day incidents where you hesitate to say or do something. If the thought of saying or doing does not arise, there is no problem at all, and you continue with your life as usual.

**Consider it as a problem only when you WANT to say or do something, and then refrain from saying or doing.**

Many times, we justify our behavior of not doing or saying things through intellectual rationalization. Think about all those instances of rationalization and identify the fears. You might feel that these little hesitations and self-restraint won't make much difference to you. But overcoming these fears will open new opportunities for you. So, decide to overcome these day-to-day fears, devise and try out EXPERIMENTs accordingly.

Some of the common major fears I can think of are:

- Fear of Death
- Fear of losing loved ones
- Fear of losing respect/love
- Fear of losing the job
- Fear of losing your wealth

Let us now look at the top item from the above list - "Fear of Death". For all other fears on the list, you need to apply a rational evaluation of options and take appropriate steps.

## The Fear of Death

As we all know death is a certainty. The advances in science and medicine can prolong our lives. But, as of now, we do not see a way to overcome death. Today life expectancy has increased, and we now see people living beyond 90 years. People 90+ years also want to be alive a few more years. It is an instinct that we want to extend our life as much as possible. Recollecting Step #2 (***Nature demands that we live our full life, and allow our species to continue***), living the full life is desired. The question now is, "What is a full life?".

The ancient scriptures have identified various phases of life. We can classify human life into 3 main phases:

1. Growing up to be an Adult
2. Raising the family
3. Old age

The 1st phase is spent on acquiring skills for livelihood. The 2nd phase is spent raising the family and ensuring that the progeny develops the necessary skills to be independent. The 3rd phase is the time for retirement from active life and to stay content with what one has achieved. Health permitting, one can lead an active life even at the ripe old age of 90. But, as per nature, we can expect our body to give in to decay, and accordingly, we should plan our activities. If you are fortunate, your children might support you in your old age or some other paid younger generation might fulfill that responsibility. Our main responsibility in life is to ensure the next generation is capable of surviving, protecting, and procreating. Once our progeny reaches that stage, we are done with our responsibility and should be ready to die at any time. As you know death is inevitable, we should accept the fact that we will die certainly one day and prepare mentally for the same.

The first step towards overcoming "the fear of death" is to embrace the fact of natural death in old age. The next step is facing the fear of unnatural death - due to a disease such as Coronavirus (COVID-19) infection, due to an accident, due to a terrorist attack, etc. These are real dangers, and you need to take proper precautions after evaluating the options available to you. This fear increases many folds if you are responsible for the well-being of others in your family. It is natural to be worried about the financial support and the emotional support they lose, in the event of your death. As a responsible parent/guardian, you should do everything possible in your control to make your dependents emotionally as well as financially independent. This, in turn, will reduce your fear and anxiety about your death.

With the advances in medicine and technology, old people as well as critically ill patients are kept alive for longer periods. It has reached such a stage that some of them are voluntarily giving up their life. This voluntary action is known as euthanasia. It is legal in a few countries in the world such as the Netherlands, Switzerland, and a few states in the USA. In 2017, in the Netherlands, there were around 6,600 people who opted for death by euthanasia. One of the famous persons who opted for euthanasia was Scientist David Goodall, aged 104. He was a London-born ecologist and botanist, living in Perth, Australia. In 2018 he flew to Switzerland to end his life peacefully. He was not terminally ill. The reason he stated for this step was "**his deteriorating quality of life**".

So, identify all your fears big or small. Prepare a plan of action for each one. Start overcoming one fear at a time. Your goal - becoming fearless.

## 2nd Pillar
## Be Assertive

I hope you know what Assertiveness is. It is neither aggressiveness nor submissiveness. It is standing up for your rights without stepping on others' rights. Many times, this behavior is misunderstood as stubbornness, being headstrong, etc.

Being assertive means expressing one's needs and rights calmly and positively without demeaning others. It is a skill that needs very good control over one's emotions. You should be able to maintain your calmness even in the face of aggressive postures by others. Great leaders such as Mahatma Gandhi and Martin Luther King Jr. have successfully used this skill to progress in their struggle against injustices. They have challenged unjust laws by mobilizing people to fight against the Governments through civil disobedience and non-cooperation. Assertiveness means protecting your rights while respecting other's rights.

How Assertive are you?

- Can you stand up for your rights?
- Can you convey your views and ideas without compromise?
- Can you say 'No' when you want to say?
- Can you express your dissatisfaction calmly?
- In short, can you take a stand for what you consider right even when all others think otherwise?

All the above questions might appear to be in the context of public protest. When it comes to your happiness, you have to pose those questions in the context of day-to-day living. You need to answer those questions by thinking about the interactions that you have daily with your family members, friends, colleagues, etc. It includes the ability to accept mistakes openly, listen to others with an open mind to assess their rightfulness and express appreciation without bias. In a few cases, you may not be able to come to an agreement with others about a point of view. It is okay. Your perspectives may be different. Everyone may be right in their perspective. In these situations, the best thing one can do is to "Agree to disagree".

One of the attitudes that come in the way of becoming assertive is "**Trying to please others**". People may develop the habit of pleasing others at their own expense. As a responsible adult, you are not supposed to cause unhappiness knowingly. But it does not mean that you need to be a victim of others' misdeeds. People who were brainwashed to be "good people" or who want to be seen as "good people", get into this trap of pleasing others at their own cost. Be ***selfishk***, call out if people start stepping on your rights. Especially in close relationships such as husband-wife, one partner might shower so much love and affection that the other chokes. In the garb of caring, they exercise their control over you. Even though you are aware of your wants, needs, and preferences you might end up toeing the line of the other just to please or not to hurt. If you are assertive, you will calmly communicate your wants and make every effort to explain the same to your partner. Initially, you will find it difficult as the other person may construe it as rejecting the love, affection, and caring shown to you. A simple example is having tea or coffee offered by your partner every day, even though you don't like that brand. If you are not assertive, you might be behaving in the same way i.e., trying to please others, with your kids, other family members, and friends; finally ending up feeling victimized.

The other factor that stops you from becoming assertive is "**Fear**". Whenever you want to show your assertiveness, others will try their best to control you. For example, when you want to exercise your rights at your office, the management might consider it as insubordination and threaten you with dire consequences. Another example could be your partner or family members threatening to withdraw love and affection. This will create fear, and you might stop being assertive. So, to become assertive you must learn to overcome fears. One common fear that holds back people from expressing their opinions is, "What would others think?". Remind yourself of **Step #6 - "*Be Open. Let Others Know You*"**. Being open helps you grow. But most importantly, realize that everybody is very busy with his/her world. Even if they criticize or disapprove of you, they may not bother to remember it. So, as far as you are clear in your conscience, you need not worry. Do what you consider is right!

By becoming assertive,

- You will not get victimized,
- You will not feel the stress of pleasing others,
- You will be able to take care of your needs better,

- You will be able to stand up for others' rights too.

To stand up for others' rights, you need to control those who make others' lives unhappy. The skill of assertiveness is essential for this. As stated above, you need to learn to be fearless to become assertive. When you decide to exhibit your assertiveness, the biggest challenge is to maintain calm in the face of provocation. To illustrate this difficulty, let me share with you two of my experiences.

**Incident #01:**

> *This incident happened while we were abroad executing a software project for a client. All of us traveled to this country leaving our families behind. It was decided that the family members could join us later. As the project progressed, the time had come to discuss the modalities of bringing our families to stay with us. In that discussion, our project manager opposed the idea of a family reunion. And openly threw a challenge that whoever wants to reunite with their family should decide at that moment and he would take appropriate action. He was hinting that he would cut short the abroad stay of that employee and send him back to his home country. For all of us, working abroad was an opportunity to make some additional money and to gain valuable experience. But I felt I was being taken for a ride. So, I decided to voice my opinion and expressed my wish to unite with my family. As my manager was not expecting this response, he got visibly upset and started shaking with anger. He shouted at the top of his voice that he would pack me off the next*

*day. To that, I calmly asked him if he could send me the same day, instead of the next day. This further angered him, and the rest of the team had a tough time calming him down. But the next day, a decision was taken to allow the families to join us abroad.*

**Incident #02:**

*It was many years back. I and my mother hired an Auto (3-wheeler Taxi) to go to our house. Before getting into the Auto, I gave the directions to the driver, and he agreed to the trip. He also agreed to take the exact fare amount that the Auto-meter shows. But after reaching our house, he demanded additional money over and above the fare. As I was practicing assertiveness, I politely refused to pay the extra money. But the Auto-driver insisted that I pay him the money. I again explained that as per the agreement, I would be paying only the fare the meter shows. Hearing this, the driver got very angry and created a scene. He abused me and my mother loudly. A few people gathered around. Looking at all this, my mother said "Just for some money, do we have to bear all these abuses? See how many people have gathered. It is so embarrassing. Give him that extra money". I told my mom that we need not feel bad as we have not done anything wrong. And asked her to go inside the house and I stood my ground. As I refused to pay extra, the Auto-driver left in frustration while abusing me further.*

I hope you get a sense of control that we need if we have to express our assertiveness. The other people will try every technique in the world to provoke you, arouse anger in you, and make you aggressive. The challenge is to remain calm, and not do anything wrong while holding on to your point of view. When it comes to practicing assertiveness, your focus is neither on the money nor on the importance of the issue, it is on the principles or ideals that you believe in and that you want to uphold.

## 3rd Pillar
## Manage Expectations

As we know, it is impossible not to have expectations. Having expectations of outcomes and having expectations of others makes our lives easy. These are beliefs about what may happen in the future, thus guiding our behavior. Typically, you arrive at expectations based on your previous experiences. Expectations help us if we assess them before we take any action. Based on the expectations that we have; we can devise our strategies to meet our goals. Thus, having reasonable expectations helps us in making our daily decisions easy.

The problem arises only when we have unreasonable expectations of outcomes. Very low expectations can lead to a pessimistic attitude, thus leading to low self-esteem and low self-confidence. On the other hand, very high expectations can make people put in less than the required effort thus making them miss their goals. A realistic expectation based on past experiences will motivate people to put in the required effort to realize their dreams.

In a normal situation, we tend to feel happy if the outcome is better than our expectations. For example, let us say we are waiting in a queue to get served and we were told that our turn will come after 45 minutes. If we are served, say, in 40 minutes, we feel happy. Instead, if we were told that our waiting time would be 30 minutes and if we were served in 35 minutes, we might feel unhappy. Even though in the 2nd situation we were served 5 minutes early, we might still feel unhappy. You might have noticed this in theme parks. Usually, they post the waiting time to be much longer than the actual time it might take.

In brief, your happiness or unhappiness at an event is based on the difference between your Expectations and the Realization. You feel happy if the Realization is more than the Expectation, and unhappy if it is less. If you observe your unhappy moments closely, many of them will be due to outcomes not meeting your expectations, or you not meeting others' expectations.

To stay happy and not get disappointed, you must manage your expectations. It involves:

1. **Having reasonable expectations from others, and of outcomes**
2. **Setting reasonable expectations for others**

Let us look at an example for the 2nd point above – Setting reasonable expectations for others. Let us say, you promised a friend or your partner that you would meet that person at a certain time, but you failed to honor that promise. What will happen? Your friend/partner gets disappointed and that can lead to an unhappy moment for you.

### 1. Have Reasonable Expectations from Others and of Outcomes:

The expectations that you have should be based on the facts, capabilities, and previous experiences. Many people mistake expectations for goals. Especially, parents get into serious disappointment when they have high expectations of their children without really assessing the children's capabilities. This leads to unwarranted stress on children as they struggle to meet the expectations of their parents. This stress can lead to the development of low self-esteem in children, and they may become rebellious too.

Instead of having high expectations, parents should set goals for their children after making a realistic assessment. The goals can be made a little challenging to motivate the kids. If a goal appears reasonable, it makes people put extra effort into achieving the same. It applies to your own goals too. You should not get into the trap of comparisons. When you compare yourself to others, you should also compare the environment, availability of resources, capabilities, and the effort you have to put in.

When it comes to expectations from others, many times we assume an implicit contract. These assumptions can cause havoc in a close relationship such as marriage. Verbalizing the expectations and having an open discussion about them can help in building the relationship. If you get frustrated and disappointed with the behavior of your partner, kids, family members, and friends:

- See if they understand your expectations clearly,
- If they understand, review if the expectations are reasonable,
- If the expectations are reasonable, check if they have the capability and necessary resources,
- Despite all that, if they do not behave, you either lower your expectations or learn ways to put them in place i.e., Condition them.

Usually, people get highly disappointed, and heartbroken when their expectations are not met by their loved ones i.e., partners, or kids. Managing the expectations of your loved ones will prepare you better to handle the situations and make you feel good. Understanding the reasons behind others not meeting your expectations will help you decide your course of action. You can plan a series of experiments that start with low expectations that others can meet. As they comply you can train them to meet your higher expectations.

In the case of outcomes of your efforts, develop an attitude of focusing on the efforts required to achieve your goals, and of accepting whatever the outcome be. In every situation, based on what you want, do everything under your control and hope for the best. With this attitude, you will start appreciating the effort you have put in. As far as the outcome is concerned, you should analyze it, and learn from it for better performance in the future.

So, think about what expectations you have of others and yourself. See if they are reasonable or if you need to calibrate them. Whenever you are disappointed with others or you, check whether it is due to unreasonable expectations. Make a conscious effort to review those situations and make amends accordingly.

## 2. Set Reasonable Expectations of You:

The way you may assume what to expect from others, others might also do the same about you. They may be assuming many things about you, and what to expect from you. If their expectations of you are high, they will be disappointed and the consequences of that could be bad for you. For example, let us say your boss expects that you will be completing a very important task by a certain date. If you delay the completion of that task, it can lead to your boss's disappointment. And you might get penalized for the same.

Who is to blame?

Whoever is to be blamed, you could become the victim. So, it is in your interest to set your expectations of you clearly. Before your boss can assume what to expect from you, you should communicate clearly to him what to expect. It means it is your responsibility to discuss the task at hand and communicate when you can complete that. In case of disagreement about the completion date, you should negotiate effectively and assertively. It might help your boss see your point of view, and accordingly adjust his expectations of you.

As discussed earlier, your boss will be happy if the realization is greater than his expectations. So, you need to deliver more than you have promised. In every situation, assess your capabilities and availability of resources then promise less and deliver more.

For your happiness, you should follow the same with your close relationships too. You should communicate to your partner, kids, parents, and friends what they can expect from you. Help them understand what you can do or provide. If you are not meeting their expectations, there can be arguments leading to discord. It is desirable to bring clarity for all about what to expect from you. Again here, your assertiveness will help you a lot in communicating your views without any fear. Even though you might have felt uncomfortable at the time of discussion, it will help you lead your life happily thereafter.

Let us look at a few simple examples of setting expectations for others.

- At work: Informing your colleagues that you will look at your emails at the beginning of the day only. If there is anything urgent, they need to make a phone call.

- While you are in the office, if your family wants to talk to you over the phone: Inform them that you may not pick up their phone call as you might be busy. They should wait for you to return the call. In case of urgency, they should call you again i.e. 2nd time. If a call is made twice, you will be picking it up.

Before making any promise, make sure that you can fulfill it without fail. A promise made sets corresponding expectations of you. If you cannot meet those expectations, it can lead to mistrust. In case you are unable to fulfill a promise, you should have the courage to communicate the same to the person concerned well in advance. This self-disclosure will minimize the damage and might stop the erosion of trust. As you might know, trust is an important ingredient for positive relationships. It helps everyone in the relationship to know what is expected of each other.

# $4^{th}$ Pillar
# Practice Detachment

If you can Manage Expectations, it will help you practice Detachment. The greatest expectation people have is that of permanence. In life, we should realize everything changes over time. It can change for the better and sometimes for the worse. But change is inevitable, and we should accept it. Heraclitus, a Greek philosopher, has been quoted as saying "Change is the only constant in life". When we don't realize this fact, we tend to get attached to people and things. Many people get attached, erroneously believing that everything continues to stay as it has been.

**Attachment to People:**

The greatest source of our unhappiness is the attachment to people. This is rooted in our irrational expectations. We expect our loved ones to be there with us in all our difficulties as well as in celebrations. Considering the realities of life, it may not always be possible for them to be with us. If you are young, you should allow your parents to have their own life. It is time for you to take charge of your life on your own and face the challenges. Take your elders' support and advice as needed, but do not expect them to solve your problems. It is your life! Apply the techniques learned in this book to your life, EXPERIMENT, and enjoy every moment of life.

If you are a parent of adult children, realize your kids have their priorities and challenges to face. And let them handle them on their own. If possible, provide the necessary support. Getting overly attached might stifle them and unnecessarily add more stress. Children give you happiness. You brought them into this world for your happiness. And they DO NOT owe anything to you. Your job is to ensure that they grow up happily to be on their own. Once they are on their own, your role as a parent is over.

The love and affection that your close family members and friends have been showering on you may not stay permanent. When you develop an Attachment with them, you feel gravely hurt when they fail to express their love as before. This is the main reason for long-term break-ups with close family members. If the same erratic behavior is displayed by a not-so-close person, you may forgive them and continue to maintain the relationship. That is because you are not so attached to them. That is the advantage of Detachment.

Pause for a minute!

Close your eyes, and check if you have cut your relationship with any of your loved ones. Make a mental list of all those people.

1. Recollect what sort of expectations you had from them.

2. If it were not for the Attachment you have with them, can you treat them differently?

3. Realize the Attachment you have. Can you go out of your way and lower your expectations?

4. Finally, what can you do now to build the relationship and rekindle the love you had?

To take the last step above,

- You have to overcome your fear of rejection,
- You should be able to convey your message assertively,
- You should Manage your Expectations,
- You should learn to Detach.

Just imagine all that happiness you have lost in these years. Think about all the unnecessary feelings of hurt and unhappiness you and the other party were going through all this time. One positive, courageous step from you can make the difference now. Just forgiving and accepting reality can add happy moments to you as well as to the other party.

Are you ready to make that move now? Best wishes!

Set this book aside and talk to the person whom you are ready to forgive.

## Attachment to Things:

I hope you might have already realized that Attachment to things is much less important when compared to Attachment to people. But in this materialistic world, some people value their things/possessions more than people. As we have seen earlier, nothing is permanent. Added to that when we die, we do not carry anything with us. You are born alone and will die alone. As Chuck Feeney is quoted as saying, “Coffins do not have pockets”.

We acquire things to make our lives easy and to live happily. By getting attached to them, we become emotionally connected and dependent on them. If some damage happens to them or if we lose them, it might cause unhappiness to us. You might have seen people being very possessive about their things. They love to demonstrate or exhibit what they have acquired. They feel happy about that. There is nothing wrong with that. It is an indication of their achievements and success. It becomes a problem if they get Attached to their possessions. I have seen people getting overly worried about a scratch on their car, dust settling on a prized possession, damage happening to their mementos, etc. Once again it is good to take care of our possessions, but if something unwarranted happens we should not lose our peace.

Again, take a moment! Think about all those things you are very Attached to.

As I mentioned in the earlier chapters, plan EXPERIMENTS to overcome your attachment to things. You can share your possessions with others. You can give away things that you no longer use. You can sell them too. See if you can still live happily without having those things that do not have any practical use for you, say for example books, mementos, etc. One of the tough Experiments in overcoming Attachment is tearing down a favorite family photo.

This Attachment to things hurts people heavily when they are in financial distress. I have come across many cases of suicide where people resorted to this extreme step even though they had sufficient funds in the form of houses and other properties. To overcome their financial crisis, they had the option of selling away their properties. But the fact that they have to do away with their prized possessions to survive has driven them to depression and suicide. If they practiced detachment, it would have been easier for them to see ways to overcome financial distress. The attachment to a certain lifestyle and social standing are also the factors contributing to this.

Apart from people and things, people do get Attached to memories and past events. These reflect in their behavior of repeatedly referring to past events and repeatedly checking photos and videos of the past. Again, there is nothing wrong as these acts give them happiness. These are positive ruminations. They keep playing them again and again. The problem arises when they do not get to replay them. It might make them unhappy. Apart from this, this Attachment to past events will come in the way of being mindful of present moments. The opportunity to create new experiences and the opportunity to live in the present moment will be lost. Every moment is a new moment, an opportunity to learn, grow, live mindfully, and enjoy.

Can you think of the ruminations that you have? See what you want to do with them.

The habits that you have concerning food, the environment you live in, and your daily routine also fall in this category of Attachment. As you progress in life, some of your old habits may not be giving you the optimal benefit. If you are Attached to them, you may not explore the new and better options that are available. It is in your interest to develop Detachment so that you can open your mind to new opportunities, new experiences and a whole new way of a happy life.

---***---

# Chapter #10
# Happiness Control Pyramid

Now that you are preparing yourself to be happy every moment, let us see how we can ensure our happiness and overall happiness in the world. Remember, every action you take can be taken by everyone in this world. So, we should keep that in mind while we develop our ability to live happily. There are four levels in this path - starting from Level 1 to Level 4. They are depicted in the next page in the form of "Happiness Control Pyramid". Your aim should be to achieve Level 1 first, and then gradually reach Level 4.

**Happiness Control Pyramid**

Let us now look at these 4 levels in detail. Even though they are depicted in a pyramid format, in reality, we all will be doing a bit of everything. This pyramid is for reminding you to focus on bottom levels first, before graduating to the next levels.

## Level 1
### Don't Make Others Unhappy

***No action of YOURS*** should hurt the other person. Refer to the "Golden Rule for Action". If your actions hurt others, you can expect someone to cause hurt to you if everyone else follows your actions. If you want to be happy you should expect others also to be happy. As far as possible you should avoid hurting others knowingly. In a way, it means ***<u>do not be selfish</u>***.

[Note: This rule changes when you reach Level 4. After you cross all 3 Levels and reach Level 4, you might hurt others intentionally to bring change in those people who are hurting others]

Be wary of the people who convey that you have hurt them by your actions. Some people might complain that you hurt them, even when your intentions are clear, and you know that there is no reason for them to feel hurt. You should be on the lookout. It might be their strategy to CONTROL you. When in doubt about your action, apply the "Golden Rule for Action". In most cases, you will find the answer.

## Level 2

### Make Your Life Happy!

Time and again many religious and spiritual gurus arrived at the idea that "Life is full of suffering, and you have to escape from it". This has created the fear of suffering, and thus fear of life. And some selfish Gurus use this fear to subjugate their followers. I hope you agree with me that "God" or "Nature" is not evil. But preachers use this fear of suffering and death, and promise you a better life, incidentally, in "After-life". And, by the way, death is not bad. Ironically, it is part of life. Recollect **Step #2 (Nature demands that we live our full life and allow our species to continue**). We will do everything possible to continue our lives despite knowing that death is a certainty.

We humans have been very successful in minimizing physical suffering. If we analyze all the developments that took place since the caveman days, man has been trying his best to ensure the continuation of a happy life. It started with physical protection and continued further on to provide comfort (far above the need). Each one of us is developing something or another to make things better for everyone - a better computer system, a better car, a better air-conditioner, and so forth.

For many of us, physical pain due to hunger, shelter or clothing is not there. But there could be pain due to health problems. And it is a proven fact that most of our physical health problems are psychosomatic i.e., physical problems due to psychological reasons. A simple basic active life can take care of REAL physical problems to a great extent.

Mental worry i.e., psychological pain is the MAJOR cause of our unhappiness. As said above, it even leads to physical health problems. Compared to all other living things, this is a unique problem for us. Some of the primates, on the top level of evolution, do display these problems. The so-called nature's gift (or God's gift) i.e., our MIND, that differentiates us from other living things itself has become the root cause of our unhappiness.

But...there is a very simple way to overcome this.

a. Every time you feel unhappy or have a bad mood, just check whether there is any physical discomfort. If it is not, there is no need to be unhappy. Measure the situation only in terms of real physical effort.

   Say, for example, someone spills a drink on you intentionally or by accident. The usual reaction could be that of repulsiveness and anger. This results in your unhappiness. If you want to teach a lesson to the other person, go ahead and do it. But, to take care of the spill on your dress, you just need to walk to the washroom and clean it. You should only be evaluating how much effort it is physically. About the psychological part, you already know how to overcome it.

b. Realize that our body is a great machine, and it has the capacity to withstand great physical stress. The "Ripley's believe it or not", "Guinness Book of Records" and "AXN" programs are testimony to it. Recognize that your mind plays the spoilsport.

c. And for real physical problems/pain, the science of Medicine has many great solutions. As I said earlier, a person can bloom and stay happy despite serious physical disabilities if she/he is so willing. Again, the great personality of Stephen Hawking comes to mind.

So, ***be selfishk.*** Make your life comfortable. Do not allow others to cause physical harm to you or hijack your mental peace. Focus on your well-being and ***selfishkly*** take up all those activities that give you happiness.

## Level 3

### Help Others Live Happily

After you gain control over your happiness, you can invest your time and energy in making others happy. ***You should attempt it, only after you gain full control over your happiness.*** If you have not mastered being happy and trying to help others to be happy, it may not be a good thing.

Watch out:

- If you are becoming dependent on this Altruism for your happiness, then you expose yourself to exploitation.
- If you help others by suffering, then there is a problem. If you apply the Golden Rule, if everyone in this world is doing the same thing as you (i.e., trying to help others to stay happy by one's suffering) then who is happy?

Do you remember the Emergency instructions in an airplane about an Oxygen mask? They advise you to put on the Oxygen mask first before helping others. You should do the same here. You should first learn to be happy before you help others to be happy. If you apply the Golden rule, the overall happiness of the world increases. Everyone who is at this level is already happy, and they are contributing to others' happiness. It might happen that you could also be receiving some additional happiness moments from others.

Why the insistence on mastering *Level* 2 before you attempt this level? Because helping others is a highly tempting act to feel happy. Helping others gives you a kick by boosting your self-esteem. It is in a way one of the easiest ways to feel superior to other fellow beings. It gives you instantaneous gratification e.g., giving alms to a beggar. And you can become dependent on this act for your happiness. If this opportunity is not there you might feel unhappy. And in many situations, you can be exploited due to this weakness. Many spiritual gurus have advocated for people to do this as it is the easiest way to show a person that he can be happy, and thus gain more following. So, if you are helping others to get your happiness, be on the watch out.

You can see the above-discussed phenomenon at work at traffic signals on Indian roads. In India, we often see beggars asking for alms and reaching out to the people who stop their vehicles at stop signals. In Western countries, you will see mostly cars and other bigger vehicles. But in India, you will find many different types and models of vehicles - Cars, 3-wheeler Auto rickshaws, 3-wheeler manual rickshaws, 2-wheeler motorbikes, bicycles, etc., each clearly showing the economic status of people. It is interesting to notice that the economically lower category people i.e., the people on bicycles and motorbikes, give alms more often than the people in cars. You can see the pride and satisfaction in them. Parting with some money is a great sacrifice for them.

For a person who learned to be happy in any situation, helping others comes naturally. It could be helping someone physically, financially, or psychologically. It won't become a burden or a sacrifice. Going by **Step #5 (No work is inferior. Enjoy every task you do. And do it to your best)**, they can enjoy every task. As they are not dependent on these tasks for their happiness, they can choose whom to help, and when to help. If you have mastered *Level 2*, you won't even remember whom you have helped, and you won't even share with anyone that you have helped. You are ready to become an anonymous helper.

Remember Chuck Feeney, the philanthropist who has donated more than $8 billion ***anonymously***? His identity was revealed during a business dispute. He is known for his frugality - living in a rented apartment, not owning a car or a house, and flying economy class (Reference: Wikipedia).

A person who has mastered staying happy in any situation can go to any extent to make others happy. He can contribute to others' well-being as a **selfless person.** He won't look forward to reciprocity, but he won't allow himself to be exploited either. He will be willing to give without any ulterior motive. The simplest thing that he can do is to make others smile. In every interaction, he makes a sincere effort to bring out a smile in other people. He can do this because he mastered control over his emotions. He can make a subtle comment or gesture to bring out a smile. And as you know a genuine smile is an indication of happiness and it is contagious too. Thus, he contributes to overall happiness.

## Level 4

### Control Those Who Make Others' Lives Unhappy

This is the final level in gaining control over happiness. As I said earlier, you should gain control over each level in the order given above. If you have crossed Level 3, you can focus on changing the behavior of persons who harm others' happiness and lives. It is a tough task. The challenge is many-fold as you need to act against these people while keeping your happiness intact. It could be fighting against the injustice caused by Government rules. It could be fighting against the atrocities committed by a few individuals. It could be fighting against the organizations that are adversely affecting public life, nature, and climate. This is the ultimate level for contributing to overall happiness in the world.

---

If you can achieve the first 2 *Levels*, you have mastered the art of staying happy. But life is not easy. The daily challenges of life make us lose control over our emotions. Apply the practical strategies that you have learned in this book for facing life's challenges.

---***---

# Chapter #11
# All About Happiness

I strongly believe that if one learns to be happy at a young age, the world will be a peaceful place for everyone. The person who has mastered being happy will not have any need to cause harm to others; and will not indulge in malpractices such as being corrupt; will not shy away from helping others. The root cause of all evils in this world is the ignorance of people, i.e. being ignorant of how to be happy. So, they go after things that cause harm to themselves as well as to others. In their earnestness, they mistake the means they adopted to reach their goal of happiness as the ultimate one. Thus, they end up focusing all their energies on those means such as amassing wealth, getting recognition, gaining power, etc.

## What is Happiness?

- The Oxford Dictionary defines it as "The state of feeling or showing pleasure".
- The science of positive psychology defines it as "Happiness in its broad sense is the label for a family of pleasant emotional states, such as joy, amusement, satisfaction, gratification, euphoria, and triumph".
- Happiness is being calm, and peaceful and being able to feel every moment, every act with equanimity.

As the above definitions highlight, happiness is *indicated* by a wide variety of positive emotions. It covers the spectrum of being calm to overtly joyous. But being happy does not mean that you should not have the emotions of sorrow, anger, etc. What it means is that you should be able to handle negative emotions with equanimity. On the contrary, if you find a person expressing joy on every occasion, you should suspect that person to be having some psychological problems.

## Current Scientific Research about Happiness

In recent years, a new branch of Psychology exclusively focused on happiness has been formed. It is called "Positive Psychology". A few years back, I took the free online course "Science of Happiness" conducted by the Greater Good Science Center (GGSC) at the University of California, Berkeley. It is commendable that the science of Psychology is attempting to unravel the existential questions through this branch of Psychology. It is interesting to note that many of the practical strategies given by this science are in line with age-old wisdom, such as being grateful and doing good.

I noticed that most of the articles on Positive Psychology are prescriptive. They tell you what acts can make you happy. These are good strategies, to begin with. They help you in the short term. As I said earlier, these strategies are akin to the preaching/rituals prescribed by religions or Gurus. Some of them are:

- Do three good things every day.
- Cultivate kindness.
- Show Gratitude, etc.

Some of the Happiness strategies are related to nature, such as:

- A awe-inspiring walk along a trail lined with tall trees, or urban settings with skyscrapers.
- Spending time at the beach etc.

All the above strategies are proven to give happiness temporarily, in the same way as rituals of a religious nature give solace to people. The focus of these studies appears to be WHAT behaviors/acts make people happy rather than HOW our mind perceives happiness. Consider this real incident:

> *One of my close friends had lost 50% of the vision in one eye. He was very depressed. And suddenly one day he called me and told me that he realized that it was not a big problem. And that he was okay with that disability. He narrated the incident that changed his perspective. While going to the office by bus, he noticed that one of his co-passengers was a blind man, and he was taking care of himself with the help of a dog. That moment made him realize that he i.e., my friend, was in a much better position compared to that blind man, and he felt happy*

*about it. Since then, he is okay with his loss of vision as there are so many people who are much worse than him. He is grateful that at least he has the vision.*

*What do you think about my friend and his feeling of happiness? There is nothing wrong with his thinking, right? We should be happy that he could reconcile with his disability.*

*If you subscribe to this concept of comparing and feeling better, you will need somebody worse than you to stay happy. Is that correct? Think! (By the way, my friend had a hearty laugh when I revealed this perspective.)*

Most of the Psychology research findings are through surveys and observations of people. They have compiled the behaviors that most people consider giving happiness. The level of happiness of these people may not be at its peak. Persons who have mastered the art of staying happy and reaching the highest levels of happiness such as bliss would be in the minority. And their methods or strategies could be completely different. What the majority considers as giving happiness may not be significant for them, on the other hand, it might hinder the process of reaching higher levels of happiness too. For example, a person who met with an accident might use crutches to ease his pain while walking, but to regain his full ability he might have to take a path of excruciating exercises. The great Bruce Lee who was condemned to bed after an accident, did the same and recovered fully to perform martial arts again. It is the same with the path to happiness. You may have to leave your crutches i.e., Happiness-giving rituals, behind to move forward.

In a few of the studies, the authors have mistakenly concluded that some behaviors lead to happiness, when in fact it was the other way around, i.e. a happy person demonstrates that behavior. For example, it was concluded that sleeping peacefully every day leads to happiness. In this, "sleeping peacefully" is a result of being happy. It is true that mimicking a particular act results in mood change to a certain extent, but it does not address the root cause of the problem.

Many of the happiness habits that are prescribed are the result of the people being happy, but not the other way around. A few of them are:

- *Happy people slow down,*
- *They have a work-life balance,*
- *They make sleep their priority etc.*

Again, here if you forcefully practice the above it can temporarily give you happiness. On the other hand, if you know how to be happy those practices become part of your life.

To gain the ultimate happiness, we cannot go by the majority rule. What gives you happiness may give repulsion to others. For example, a non-vegetarian enjoys eating meat and it gives him happiness. But the same meat might give repulsive feelings to a pure vegetarian. Let us assume that eating meat gives great happiness to most people, but prescribing Vegetarians to eat meat to stay happy is not correct. Arriving at conclusions based on the experiences of the majority of people may not be the right one.

## The Set-Point Theory of Happiness

Measuring happiness is a tough task as it means different things to different people. Scientists are still trying to figure out how to measure it objectively. Many of the measurements are based on self-report assessments. Let us look at one of the popular theories about happiness levels - the "Set-point theory of Happiness".

'The Set-Point Theory of Happiness' says, "Our *levels of happiness remain constant throughout our lives as genetics and personality traits determine our subjective well-being. During our lifetime we might experience changes in our levels of happiness due to life events but the level returns to its baseline over time.*"

As per this theory, our happiness level is affected,

a) to the extent of 50% by our genetic predisposition
b) to the extent of 10% by External circumstances
c) and 40% by our Actions & Thoughts

As we cannot control our Genetics (a), and we can only in part control our External circumstances (b), so there's only one thing left to increase our happiness i.e., our Actions and thoughts (c). Research by Sonja Lyubomirsky has shown that we can raise our "happiness baseline" but it is limited to (c) only.

I feel the conclusion that we have a "Happiness baseline" is due to the consistency of our behavior and personality. As Sonja Lyubomirsky mentioned, we can raise our happiness level by working on our "Actions and thoughts". Interestingly, with the change in "Actions & Thoughts", you can handle the outcomes of external circumstances too. As far as genetics is concerned it is debatable. Nature vs Nurture debate is an age-old one. As you might have noticed, to gain control over your happiness your personality needs to be transformed. And it is possible through the strategies that we have discussed in this book.

Thus, I do not agree with the concept that 50% of the level of happiness is determined by genetics and that only 50% of it is left for us to improve. I agree that the effort required to transform the way we think, and act will vary from individual to individual. A total transformation of the personality is required for a person to experience high levels of happiness. That is the reason why this goal of achieving happiness is a tough nut to crack. And for ages, people have been trying hard to find strategies that everyone can adopt. Unfortunately, there are no shortcuts.

The acts suggested by Positive Psychology such as 3 acts of kindness, gratitude journal, etc., do help in improving happiness for many people. I feel they are interim strategies for gaining short-term happiness. As said earlier, these acts are like crutches. Some studies concluded that the effect of these interventions lasts not more than a few months. The real happiness/ eternal happiness / the bliss is beyond these acts.

The question we should be asking is WHY do these acts make us happy? Researchers found that when you show 'gratitude' or 'perform acts of kindness' the feel-good hormone "Dopamine" is released. But the unfortunate reality is that some people get happiness by troubling and hurting others. Say, a kid gets kicked out of bullying other children. So, my question is - "When someone gets happy by beating another person or bullying another person, what type of hormones or chemicals are released?" I could not find the answer to this in the literature. I have the feeling that the same "Dopamine" might be getting released. So, in between an act and the release of the hormone "Dopamine", there is something else that we usually call feeling or emotion. A particular feeling/emotion might release a particular hormone. In the case of "Dopamine", a person feeling good/excited about a particular action might be the cause. A sadist or masochist might have learned to feel good while inflicting pain on others or self, and "Dopamine" might get released. So, the release of the hormone "Dopamine" cannot become the sole reason for advocating the practice of certain acts for happiness.

Many great thinkers, philosophers, sages, and spiritual leaders have done extensive research in this area after observing human suffering and meditating on this problem. Their teachings are not easily understandable and thus many schools have mushroomed to pass on that knowledge through various Gurus. Unfortunately, many of these Gurus demand **surrender** to achieve happiness. This one aspect of their teachings, i.e. surrendering, and having blind faith, opens opportunities for exploitation.

Philosophers and spiritual gurus tried to unravel the mystery of happiness by focusing on WHY we feel happy rather than WHAT makes us happy. Their search led them to focus on the inner world rather than the outer world. It is common knowledge that:

- There are umpteen number of situations that make people happy.
- A particular situation can generate different feelings in different people.
- The same situation faced at different times by the same person can generate different feelings.
- Conditions that are considered abysmal, inhabitable can

also make people feel happy.

The above facts have led the great thinkers to the conclusion that irrespective of the conditions outside, what goes on in one's inner world i.e., in one's mind, decides how happy a person can be. Their mantra is:

**"Control your mind,**
**to have control over your happiness".**

---***---

# Epilogue

Understanding the *Four Pillars* and mastering control over them is the key to happiness. You need to consciously work on building those Four Pillars. As you might have understood by this time, the only thing that you have FULL CONTROL over is your mind and nothing else. And I hope you will agree that you can be happy in any situation, and you don't need a reason to be happy.

1. **Decondition yourself to become Fearless.**
2. **Fearlessness helps you to become Assertive.**
3. **Assertiveness helps you to Manage Expectations effectively.**
4. **Managing Expectations helps you to develop Detachment.**

To reach this stage, you should master the technique of deconditioning i.e. EXPERIMENTING, effectively. The chapter "**Lay the Foundation**" gives you the power to develop control over your emotions, the main ingredient for happiness.

As you recollect, we have started by reviewing what happiness means to you. Later, we focused on the 7 steps that we need to cross to have clarity about life. We have looked at the 3 boulders that need to be broken. We reviewed the approaches to handling day-to-day life challenges. And finally zeroed in on the technique "Experiment", to decondition and help you gain your freedom. Let us now look at how to put all this into practice.

## Developing Self-Mastery, and Gaining Personal Freedom

Start working relentlessly on deconditioning yourself. It will lead to Personal Freedom, where you are the master of your actions and destiny. Make a conscious decision to follow the actions detailed below:

1. **Practice being *selfishk*.** Do not allow others' behavior to take away your happiness. Let them shout, let them show anger, let them insult you, but do not let them take away your power to stay calm. Practice slow-deep-breathing. Even if you have to toe their line and perform a task that you don't like, do it while staying calm. Use that situation to think about how you can change/handle it next time.

   As you know being ***selfishk*** means taking care of yourself without hurting others. So, take time out for yourself without any guilt feelings. Use that time to recharge yourself and enjoy yourself. Take up those activities that you like.

2. **Avoid multi-tasking and embrace Time-boxing:** Whatever the stage of life we are in, we must handle multiple things all the time. Plan your tasks and allocate time for each of them. Take up one task at a time during its allotted time. Focus fully on that one task, in other words, become *Mindful*, and experience *Flow.*

3. **Always, remember the "Pause and Choose" idea**. In day-to-day interactions, practice to Pause consciously. Take slow deep breaths. Slow down a little when you converse even if you feel there is no need to think. This behavior change gives you the power to think and choose when a situation demands. When you master it, there won't be any need to slow down in every interaction.

4. **Evaluate every situation with the 7 steps.** Every moment of our life is different. We can even say that every situation is unique. That is what makes life interesting as well as challenging. Whenever you face a challenging situation, evaluate it with the perspective of the 7 steps. Recollect the "Golden Rule for Action" [Refer to Chapter #3]. Hopefully, you will find your path.

   Think about all consequences of your action. Be prepared for the worst. Practice relaxing. Plan all your steps and focus on the current step/task on hand.

5. **Focus on Experimenting.** Identify the behavior patterns that you want to change in yourself. List them out and

apply the deconditioning technique. Start with the easy-to-correct behaviors. Be creative. Plan experiments. Try them out. Check the progress you made. If need be, devise new experiments. Continue that till you are happy with your progress. Enjoy that success. Then, move on to changing more challenging behaviors one by one to gain Self-Mastery.

6. **Build the four pillars**. Finally, focus on the four pillars. Devise Experiments to speed up the process of your learning. Observe the improvements in you; celebrate ***selfishkly*** every small gain that adds to your power. It will be a long path. So, it is prudent to observe every small gain you make. Enjoy the benefits that accompany these gains. I am sure you will love the process and enjoy every step of this journey to your Personal Freedom.

---

Apply the techniques discussed in this book to your day-to-day interactions. After a reasonable time of practice, say one month, review the progress you made. I whole-heartedly hope that you see the trend of improvement in your happiness.

Hope this book has given you the control to master your happiness. Now it is up to you to decide, how effectively and how soon you want to start living happily. It is my firm belief that if everyone learns to live happily, the world will stay in eternal peace.

Gaining emotional control can help you achieve your goals effectively, thus becoming successful in every endeavor. Being happy helps you navigate the path to your goals with much more ease and effectiveness. I hope you use this power to achieve those goals that help mankind.

**Enjoy Life!**

**---@@@---**

# Acknowledgments

I am indebted to the following family members for reviewing chapter by chapter and giving me constructive feedback.

1. Dr. M. Prabhakar - My brother-in-law
2. Sri. T. Sudhakar – My brother
3. Lt. Col. (Dr) T. Dayakar – My brother
4. Sri. T. Kishan Rao – My brother
5. Dr. T. Bhaskar Rao – My brother
6. Dr. T. Giridhar – My brother
7. Sri. M. Sudhir – My nephew

Based on their feedback, I have modified the content to make it a good read. Special thanks to my nephew Sudhir for sharing his feedback without mincing words. His frank comments pushed me to rewrite an entire chapter.

Thanks to my immediate family members for their support – my wife Kiranmai, my son Pratyush, my daughter Dr. Sanjana and my son-in-law Ravi Kammili (Vamsi).

Thanks to my 'Bava garu' Sri. Sam Prasad Kammili, and to Sri. Ravi Lolla for providing feedback after reviewing the Special Edition.


---***---

# About the Author

Thota Ramesh currently lives in Dallas, TX. He is a Counseling Psychologist by passion, and a Software Delivery head by profession. He is an accomplished speaker. His favorite topics include Enjoying life, Behavioral Transformation, Emotional Intelligence, and Stress Management.

He is a postgraduate in Business Administration and Applied Psychology. At a young age he learned Magic & Hypnotism to understand the working of the mind. He believes in educating people to see reason and to live happily. He strives to do his bit through seminars and writing articles/books. He feels the majority of human beings are good, but they allow bad things to happen as they are fearful and unassertive.

As a software professional, he had worked in many countries including the USA, UK, Zimbabwe, Egypt, Syria, Chile. His sports interests include Cricket, Table Tennis, and Snooker. And he loves playing Bridge with his brothers.

---***---

# Other Books by the Author

(Available at www.amazon.com)

## Teamwork & Indian Culture

A Practical Guide for Working with Indians

**Understand Indian Culture, and Communicate effectively with Indians**

This book is about Indian Culture, focusing on workplace behavior. This book acts as a cross-cultural trainer for non-Indians. If you are visiting India for business, it prepares you well to enjoy your trip. This is a good companion book to India Travel Guide. **This Revised edition includes a chapter on "Chalta-hai" attitude of Indians.**

It explains the reasons for the typical aspects of Indian Culture while focusing on the Teamwork culture in India. **It guides people who want to interact with Indians effectively.** This book analyzes the impact of Indian Culture on the workplace behavior of Indians. It provides insight into how that behavior evolved, and also suggests techniques to overcome the negative influence of those behavior patterns.

**These cross-cultural ideas are communicated through a fictitious story revolving around an American, managing a software team in India.** "John, a young American manager from the IT department of a major retail chain, comes to India to execute an IT project. This is the first overseas assignment for John. Dheeraj, Program Manager at India office, has been entrusted with the responsibility of helping and guiding John.

**Know the Indian Culture and *Enjoy Working with Indians!***

---***---

## Daily Life in Indian Culture

An Insightful Guide to Customs & Traditions of India

**Gain insights into the Indian way of life and Enjoy Your India Travel**

This book helps you overcome the Indian cultural barriers and enjoy your India Travel. You get the best experience of Indian culture, through the character of John. This story of John makes you feel, relate, understand, and experience the way Indians live. If you are traveling to India, this book will help you a lot in getting along with Indians and enjoying India. It takes you through the real-life situations of India.

Everything that you need to know to understand the customs, traditions, and rituals of India is presented in this book. The various aspects of Indian Culture are explained in a rational &

experiential way. This book vividly presents the situations and scenarios that John has faced.

"John returns to America, after six months of stay in India, as a positively transformed person. His relationship with his live-in girlfriend changes for better. He recounts all that he experienced during his stay in India and the insights he got."

This book goes beyond the typical dos & don'ts. It provides an insight into the practicality of rituals, and into the typical life philosophy of Indians - including the way Indians look at life and happiness. It helps you understand the psyche of Indians and provides explanation for all the behavior that is unique to Indians.

**Take this virtual tour with John and Enjoy India Travel!**

--***--

# NOTES

www.ingramcontent.com/pod-product-compliance
Lightning Source LLC
LaVergne TN
LVHW091321150826
845673LV00006B/1724

*9798886842098*